T0195706

RADICAL

TRANSFORMATIONS

SEEDS OF PROMISE

PEARLINE RICHARDSON

WESTBOW
PRESS®
A DIVISION OF THOMAS NELSON
& ZONDERVAN

Copyright © 2020 Pearline Richardson.

All rights reserved. No part of this book may be used or reproduced by
any means, graphic, electronic, or mechanical, including photocopying,
recording, taping or by any information storage retrieval system
without the written permission of the author except in the case
of brief quotations embodied in critical articles and reviews.

This book is a work of non-fiction. Unless otherwise noted, the author
and the publisher make no explicit guarantees as to the accuracy of
the information contained in this book and in some cases, names
of people and places have been altered to protect their privacy.

WestBow Press books may be ordered through booksellers or by contacting:

WestBow Press
A Division of Thomas Nelson & Zondervan
1663 Liberty Drive
Bloomington, IN 47403
www.westbowpress.com
1 (866) 928-1240

Because of the dynamic nature of the Internet, any web addresses or
links contained in this book may have changed since publication and
may no longer be valid. The views expressed in this work are solely those
of the author and do not necessarily reflect the views of the publisher,
and the publisher hereby disclaims any responsibility for them.

Any people depicted in stock imagery provided by Getty Images are models,
and such images are being used for illustrative purposes only.
Certain stock imagery © Getty Images.

Scripture quotations taken from The Holy Bible,
New International Version® NIV®
Copyright © 1973 1978 1984 2011 by Biblica, Inc. TM.
Used by permission. All rights reserved worldwide.

ISBN: 978-1-9736-8858-7 (sc)
ISBN: 978-1-9736-8857-0 (e)

Library of Congress Control Number: 2020904838

Print information available on the last page.

WestBow Press rev. date: 5/13/2020

CONTENTS

Freebasing My Jesus

He came one night and swept me up
with a passion that would not stop
like the tight hug of wee toddler
hanging on with joy and refusing to let go
just begging with giggles
to be close and never put down.

That is my Lord.
Lover of my soul
Keeper of my heart
Holder of my hand
Companion in my walk...

beside me
before me
behind me...
hemming me in with safety and love.

My Lords sweet love.
It brought me solace from heart ache
relief from the brutality of anxiety.
He gave me sanctuary when I was abandoned
and cast away like a ratty shoe...

He stood guard with compassion
while I wiped rivers of tears
I felt His warm hand at my neck
as I knelt in anguished prayer.

Always He was there whispering
His promises of a future and
even more...
now.

When I was ready.

In those moments I learned that
I had only to look at Him
truly gaze upon His countenance and
there I would find
a friend
a Counselor
a Father
my Savior.

I would find my path again
and I did.

Here, where word is formed
I have found the pipeline to my God.
My conduit
Freebasing my Jesus

as I am refined by the one true Gods fire
and cooled by His breath.

May the words of my mouth
and the deeds of my hands
bring Glory to God and
point in the only direction He is.

~Amen

FOREWORD

There's a moving picture that comes to my mind of the incredible ripple effect that happens with accepting Jesus as our Lord and Savior. A single, smooth stone, dropped in a crystal, clear water pond deep in the mountains, sending out a ripple in all directions. That one ripple induces another, and another and another and it keeps on going...

Those ripples continue well beyond what we can see with the naked eye. They are viewable on the surface but they are not exclusive to surface only. They are impacting beneath the surface as well. The ripple effect of a heart for Christ is more than just on the individual but exponentially extends to every single person within the sphere of a saved individual.

"Freely you have received, freely give." Matthew 10:8b What a blessing it is to have received God's grace and then the privilege to extend it to others.

Matthew 28:18-20 *"Then Jesus came to them and said, 'All authority in heaven and on earth has been given to me. Therefore, go and make disciples of all nations, baptizing them in the name of the Father and of the Son and of the Holy Spirit, and teaching them to obey everything I have commanded you. And surely, I am with you always, to the very end of the age.'*

Father,
I thank you
for every part of this journey with you.
May your blessings abound on the mind
and heart of every person who seeks you.
May these testimonies find soft hearts
yearning for you
and spark renewed hope.
May there be an increased movement
in all lives to experience an encounter with you.
 May your promise of renewal be profound;
Spreading far and wide
to the nations of the world.

~Amen

HOPE IN SILENCE

I called him the "boy in blue." That was all that ever needed to be said. A soft-spoken, Hispanic who stood over 6 feet tall and weighed in at well over 250lbs at 17 years of age, he openly represented his gang affiliation. His families' affiliation was well known as were their activities. He was known by all: student and staff alike. While he had a naturally happy personality, he was not to ever be underestimated. He was respected as a fighter in the ring and out. His hands were stunningly rugged. They bore the evidence of years of fighting. Scars all over and his knuckles were enlarged and calloused from repeated contact on some poor opponent.

I liked him. I like most teenagers and he was a delight to me; always ready to laugh he followed a strict code of personal conduct. He took care of his "family". Some days I walked beside him, other days I led him to an office for his next meeting with an administrator or someone from law enforcement. He always had a smile for me.

"Miss!"

"How are you today, Jose?"

"Good, Miss. You?"

"I'm doing good. You staying out of trouble?"

Smirking, he looked back at me and replied, "Yes…" I chuckled and knew better.

Jose' responded to my directives when I gave them. Like most struggling students, Jose,' responded with respect to, respect. Jesus tells us in Luke 6:31 *"Do to others as you would have them do to you."* Wise Solomon speaks to us repeatedly of our words. Proverbs 15:1 says, *"A gentle answer turns away wrath, but a harsh word stirs up anger."*

From the very first contact, how we physically position and posture ourselves to the first words spoken to another, we have the ability to set the tone for every encounter thereafter. Each encounter is not just about the moment you are in with a youth but, rather each of the moments ahead as well. Reconciliation together at the end of a contact or situation goes a long way to easing into the next encounter. The moments are always connected. After all, we are building relationships and looking for the moments when God can speak from you and touch the one in front of you. Sometimes that touch can be had in silence. Sometimes the gentleness IS silence.

1 Peter 3:4 *"Rather, it should be that of your inner
self, the unfading beauty of a gentle and quiet
spirit, which is of great worth in God's sight."*

There is peace to be gained in the silence we give. I know
at times I just want someone to be next to me. I don't always
need advice but certainly having a person stand with me can
be encouraging.

Up until the last several weeks, Jose was a student in our
building, his smile was there. It saddened me to see it slowly
disappear. It's a very different situation once youth become
adults. The, much looked forward to, 18th birthday brings
significant change with it. Some good. Some not so good. In
Jose's case, like many others, it meant that juvenile detention
was no longer an option. As an adult any new arrest would
put him in jail.

Jose' was stuck. His violations list was not short and
with his background of fighting and notoriety, he was a
target. The pressure was on him from within our building
and on the streets to perform. There were those pushing
his buttons. There was also another young man with a rival
gang join the ranks within our building. From day one he
circled and taunted Jose. Jose repeatedly attempted to steer
clear. Over and over again he walked away from the young
man. The boys had a few minor verbal altercations but with
each one they became increasingly more volatile.

Jose' was warned by all that any more fights and he

would be arrested. Unlike the new student Jose' was 18. The new student was only 16. A physical altercation would earn Jose' a long walk out of our building in cuffs.

The day finally came when the inevitable happened. The two boys got loud and somebody lunged. Security broke it up before it became a full contact fight but not soon enough. The boys ended up in different offices. Administration was angry. The halls had been tense for days with rising tensions between the rivals. While those with any authority were hashing their way through decisions, regarding suspending these two boys from school, I was sent to join Jose'.

My heart was heavy as I walked down the long hall to where Jose' was waiting for the outcome of his criminal charges. As I walked, I prayed. Not many words. I worked at giving my heavy heart to God. I visualized cupping my hands and reaching out with them as if to hand off what my hands cradled: the burden of sadness, disappointment, frustration and helplessness. The closer I got to the staff room where Jose' was being held, the more I felt, "Be with him" Nothing more than that. I felt just the sense of quietness and to, "Be with him".

As I unlocked the door and walked in the room, you could feel anger and frustration being contained. The man in the room stood next to Jose, berating and condemning him. Jose', radiating tension while his hands were resting, clasped on the table top. He stared; not talking; rigid.

Frustrated, by Jose's refusal to speak, the man left. I

stood for a second taking in the moment and went to sit across the table from Jose. He glanced at me and I could tell he was expecting more berating. I slowly sat down, took a deep breath and let it out. Quieting my own spirit I continued to sit, relaxed. I waited. Content to be sitting with him and willing my calmness to be tangible.

After a couple of minutes Jose' glanced up at me; defensively and questioningly. I smiled gently, "I am just gonna sit with you. You don't have to wait alone. We'll do it together."

There is *"A time to be silent and a time to speak"* Ecclesiastes 3:7b

And so…we sat. With each breath his breathing became deeper and his shoulders began to slowly drop.

His hands relaxed their rigid hold and eventually let go of each other. He began to feel again. Something more than frustration…maybe sadness. His eyes took on regret. We sat at that table for some time. Neither of us said anything. There was no need to.

When we get out of the way we allow our Father in heaven to work through us. We become the vessel by which HE speaks to the hearts who need. Jose' did not need words from me. He already knew what he was in for. There was nothing I could do to stop what was ahead for him or even change it. My hope was that by providing him a quiet space that God could speak to his heart all the things I never could. Jose' just needed to have a moment of emotional safety. A moment of quiet in the midst of his personal storm.

The time came where I could tell by the radio traffic in my ear piece they would be coming for Jose'. That was when I finally spoke again, softly. "Jose'…" He looked at me with kindness.

"No matter what happens today you will be ok. This is not the end and you will be ok." He nodded at me. "They'll be here soon." He kept slowly nodding and looked down at the table. He did not get tense again but he sat up straighter, his proud shoulders returned. He was ready.

When they came for him he stood up with confidence and walked to the door and just before he walked out he turned to me and simply said, "Thank you, miss."

> *"But those who hope in the Lord will*
> *renew their strength."* Isaiah 40:31

One of the most beautiful testimonies we have of Christ and his graciousness is the story of him and the woman who was caught in adultery.

John 8: 2-11 *"At dawn he appeared again in the temple courts, where all the people gathered around him, and he sat down to teach them. The teachers of the law and the Pharisees brought in a woman caught in adultery. They made her stand before the group and said to Jesus, "Teacher, this woman was caught in the act of adultery. In the Law Moses commanded us to stone such women. Now what do you say?" They were using this question as a trap, in order to have a basis for accusing him."*

Silence

"But Jesus bent down and started to write on the ground with his finger."

How long did he remain silent, calmly bent down writing? Long enough they became insistent.

"When they kept on questioning him, he straightened up and said to them, "'Let any one of you who is without sin be the first to throw a stone at her.'"

Silence

"Again, he stooped down and wrote on the ground. At this, those who heard began to go away one at a time, the older ones first, until only Jesus was left, with the woman still standing there."

Again, how long did Jesus remain silent, calmly waiting as the audience was processing what Jesus had said? Some minutes must have passed till it was just Jesus and the woman. Jesus had effectively removed the audience and restored dignity to the woman by creating a moment that he could speak directly and intimately, straight to the heart of the matter.

"Jesus straightened up and asked her, 'Woman, where are they? Has no one condemned you?'"

"No one, sir," she said.
"Then, neither do I condemn you," Jesus declared. "Go now and leave your life of sin."

There are so many commentaries on this event in Jesus's ministry. It is a beautiful moment of grace and mercy. From the arrival of the Pharisees, Jesus was listening. Jesus was always listening to the Holy Spirit. We know, and I cannot help but think, that this is one of those rare glimpses we have of the interaction between the Father and the Son.

Everything about this moment spoke humility and grace from Jesus. Jesus quieted himself and took a posture of submission by physically lowering himself to the ground. Jesus humbled himself to his Father in Heaven by seeking counsel from the Holy Spirit. Remember, Jesus only did what he saw the Father doing and said what He heard his Father saying. In doing so, Jesus also humbled himself to the woman who stood ready to be condemned by him. By lowering himself to a position on the ground, Jesus was speaking first with body language.

Many have wondered what Jesus was writing in the dirt. He was writing a monumental moment in history of gentleness, kindness and grace. The 'what' Jesus wrote is not as significant as the fact that he wrote. Jesus used his body language, posturing and temperament to de-escalate the condemning attitude of the Pharisees toward the woman. In re-directing the attention of the Pharisees to themselves they became frustrated that Jesus was not answering them.

This was a crises moment in the woman's life! She was likely battered and bruised; exposed, humiliated and shamed. She was expecting and waiting to be stoned. Jesus defused the toxic and condemning air of hate and "look at her!" attitude and successfully re-directed it to influencing the Pharisees awareness of themselves. In essence, He used their pride to his advantage and in doing so the amazing happened. He took the heat off the woman and set the stage for those accusing to look at their lives. I cannot help but wonder how aware the woman was of Jesus' every move and breath. She hung on his every word and he knew she was. He was so gentle with her knowing that and so careful to not condemn but bring the Fathers kindness. He was slow and still, and in his silence the hearts of those who heard him, shifted.

Can you imagine the woman's whole world altering in the moments she stood there watching as one by one the audience left, knowing they were not going to throw a single stone? Can you imagine her terror slowly turning to profound relief? Can you imagine her emotions as she looked at this man, named Jesus, who knelt in the dirt slowly tracing his finger through it all the while his whole attention was on her? She knew it. She would have felt it.

This man that could have had her killed, or at the least scorned her but instead, treated her with dignity.

Sometimes we need the wisdom to be quiet.
I have had several beautiful moments where I
was blessed to see the power of silence.

Alleluia...you are mine
Creator of all
Alleluia…El Shaddai'
to my knees I fall.

Alleluia...hands lifted high
In worship of you.
Alleluia...Alleluia
Blessed are you my King

You are Adonai
You are worthy
You are mine
Always and forever more
Mine...

FOUNDATIONS

"A Security Specialist at a high school? Wow! What's that like?"

Inevitably, I receive more questions of fascination, mixed with a bit of skepticism, when asked what my job is. I give a brief explanation as best as I can, "Sadly, we can thank Dylan Klebold and Eric Harris for my occupation. The Columbine shootings birthed my job." The primary situation we train for is a 'shooter in the building' scenario however, on an average day, anything goes. Students skip, throw tantrums, have fender benders on campus, get high. It's normal to deal with bullying, theft or drugs on a daily basis and on a rough day, assault and any other violent activity. Anything that happens in the life of a youth can, and often does, happen while in school.

The seriousness of my reply is usually successful at opening the eyes of those that think of my job as nothing more than babysitting. Sometimes it takes a bit more explanation but there are always more questions to follow.

Some just want to hear about drugs and gangs. Others want to hear about "crazy stuff teenagers do". (Fart machines, fuzzy dice and stories of students getting the munchies brings chuckles.) Transgenders, cross dressing, bathroom sharing and the increase in "self-harm" behaviors come up. Most are fascinated by how technology in the hands of teenagers plays a huge part in the job with regards to bullying and sexual exploitation and all are blown away by the reminder that violent crimes against minors happen.

I am often asked, "How did you end up in that job?" and always my reply is, "I love teenagers. I have been working with them for 27 years and I cannot imagine doing anything else."

I have known since the age of 13 that I would spend my life dedicated to youth. The passion for others began when a junior high friend was murdered and my heart has been devoted since. Time and again I have been humbled by profound blessings from so many young lives and also, through deep tragedy and loss.

And here I am, age 46, with a heart that burns with passion, for the lost and hurting. The fire for youth stems from the fact they are dependent on adults in their life and are so directly impacted by the choices of those who are to be responsible for them. They need us. They need us to stand in the gap. They need our voices. They need our time. They need our leadership. They need our encouragement. Simply put: they need.

They need Jesus. They need to know His love and that He loves them perfectly.

Some years ago, I was searching for a worship song to accompany my prayer time and I came across a worship session online. The lead vocals were two very prophetic women; one was singing. She let her heart for the Lord lead her worship and she softly sang the simple phrase, "It all begins and ends with love…"

It all begins and ends with love…

Our Lords heart for us is, His love. He created us with design and purpose because He loves us. Everything in creation He gifted to us because He loves us. His intention is our success and He loves' us with perfection seeking only to love on us and, through us. His delight is in our discovery of all He has created for us.

God.

Is.

Love.

"Love is patient and kind; love does not envy or boast; it is not arrogant or rude. It does not insist on its own way; it is not irritable or resentful; it does not rejoice at wrongdoing, but rejoices with the truth. Love bears all things, believes all things, hopes all things, endures all things. Love never ends." 1 Corinthians 13:4-8a

As His people, His love becomes our love, for others. Agape'. His single-minded purpose for us is to love us.

Especially when we step out of his design for us. Then, in the aftermath we have to deal with whatever consequences arise from our behaviors or thought processes. Those moments are when His love is most radiant and He bestows on us grace. The Lord waits for us in those moments to walk with us; to speak to us and share His heart on the matter.

The Fathers heart is to minister to us as we walk in this world. Our calling from the Father is to have the same heart for others as He has for us. He gives to us, so we freely can give to others. The same Christlike giving is evidenced as others pour into our own lives or, when we pour into others.

In my early teens I was blessed to have a few individuals minister and pour into me. My own siblings, much older than I, were an integral part of my upbringing. They stood to bridge gaps and provide protection for me. I can say with absolute confidence that my siblings were the light in the darkness of my childhood. Three older brothers and one sister, 10-17 years older than I had a huge impact on my life. They were my babysitters and parents. They played with me, bandaged my injuries, disciplined me when I needed it, broke eggs over my head, gave me a few black eyes (accidentally of course), taught me to climb trees, played football with me and by with me I mean I WAS the ball. Ya, they taught me to be sassy and not afraid of anything. All lessons that saved me many times. There was never any doubt that I was protected.

Additionally, there were two men who loved on me in my

teen years like a father would. One was an elder of the church I attended. He greeted me every Sunday with a hug and kind words. His sincerity was heartfelt and tangible to me. He was a street-smart man and recognized my own sassiness. There was no fooling him and I respected him for it.

The other was a man that eventually became my father-in-law. Again, a savvy man who knew the ways of the world and was very direct in speech. This kind man was my father-in-law for nearly 20 years. He was a blessing to me personally and through him I learned what it was to be adopted into an adults' heart. He set the example for me of what it was to love in ways a parent would to a youth that was not his own. I learned what that sounded like, felt like and looked like. He was real about his own walk with the Lord and how he grew as a Christian. He gave his heart to the Lord a few years after I met him. My father-in-law was a man that could sometimes be a little rough around the edges, but always very loving. His spiritual transformation is one that I watched over the span of many years. I am forever thankful that God gifted me the opportunity to learn from him. Having grown up with no father both of these men impacted my life.

Another individual who was pivotal in my teen years was a delightful woman who also became my grandmother-in-law. She was a spiritual rock of grace and faith. I have met few men, or women, who were as tapped into the power of the Holy Spirit as was this amazing woman. Her gentleness and kindness enveloped her everywhere she went. Despite chronic pain she never uttered one word of complaint. Her personal grit set the standard by which I have measured my own physical endurance to run the race God has me in. I ask myself, "Am I running with the same dignity?" Her praise of the Lord in all circumstances kept her upright and smiling when most others would have succumbed.

These individuals laid the foundation in my life by which I built my ministry on. Through them I was loved, encouraged and the fire was fanned to pour the same care into others. As much as I was impacted by such loving people there is wisdom in looking to who they reflected and they reflected the love of Jesus.

Jesus portrayed the perfect model of life. He loved with kindness and taught with compassion. Jesus was passionate about teaching and modeling a life ministering to others. Ministry is holding the hands of others because Christ held ours. Ministry is serving the needs of others in whatever area of their life they are experiencing need because Christ first served us and still does. Ministering to another does not require a request or permission. It is simply done because it is good. Because it is kind. Because it is love. It is Gods' love through us.

Let us rise
under your shelter, Father.
The sheer radiance
of the Savior,
like the morning dawn
bringing peace
to all hearts.

LOVE THEM LIKE YOUR OWN

Early on in my personal ministry, in my early 20's, I made a commitment to fulfill whatever role God placed on me for a youth for whatever time He needed me to fill it. Most often it was Mentor. Sometimes it was Sister, Aunt, Mother. (Ya, sometimes all that is needed is a mom.) Sometimes it was Mediator or Intercessor. I have learned how to recognize and shift from one role to another depending on the needs of the situation. I didn't always do it well. Especially when I was younger. Thankfully, God is patient and continues to teach me.

I don't know when I first prayed, "Lord, who do I need to be?" In the moment, whatever the crises, it just happens.

I remember one of the earliest times it was impressed upon me to do so. It was in the early 90's and I was maybe 20 years old. I was a volunteer youth worker at a church in Oregon at the time. The situation was a heated conflict transpiring in the churches' kitchen between two jr. high females and still, after 30 minutes, it was not de-escalating. Because of my age I was approaching the situation as a friend would and getting no-where. I had a plea in my heart to the Lord, "Who do I need to be?" and the instant impression returned was "sister". An older sister would have been very annoyed at her two little sisters being brats. Well, I was certainly annoyed at them behaving like brats so I told them so, "You two need knock this off and stop being brats! Go ahead and take a look at each other and see how ridiculous this is!"

It was dead silent. They looked at me shocked. Frankly, I was a little shocked myself. However, it pretty much defused the whole thing right there much to my surprise. Here I had been trying to be diplomatic and "adult-like" on my soap box and what I had needed to do was step off the soapbox and get real. They needed to knock it off and to be told that. Point blank. This had not been the first round for these two girls and I could not help feel like it was time to leave behind the childish ways. They walked out of that kitchen some 10 minutes later smiling at each other and…never again did we have a conflict situation like that between them.

I often think that if the Holy Spirit were to manifest in the room, during a conflict, it would be as a man, lounged against the wall, arms crossed over his chest, lips slightly pursed and one eyebrow raised at what He was watching happen. If He were to speak? It would be something to the effect of: "Knock it off."

The interesting thing is I am the youngest of my siblings. Technically, I have no younger siblings to pull from experience on. Yet, for the next 10 years, after the circumstances in the kitchen, as I learned how the Lord wanted me to mentor, He called on me periodically to be a big "Sister." The Lord grew me in compassion and understanding during those times and I gained more experience in leaning in on Him to guide me through each situation. How do you step into a role you have zero experience with? I trusted in that if the Lord was directing me to be the sister then, He was also going to prepare me and speak through me.

We have the promise in Philippians 4:19 *"And my God will supply every need of yours according to his riches in glory in Christ Jesus."* It is a straight forward and wonderful promise! We can have confidence that whatever work God assigns us He is going to equip us for. Thank goodness we can stand on that promise just like Paul goes on to encourage Timothy in 2 Timothy 3:16-17, *"All Scripture is God-breathed and is useful for teaching, rebuking, correcting and training in righteousness, so that the servant of God may be thoroughly equipped for every good work."*

The Lord never sends us out without equipping us. We are never going to be in a situation or face an obstacle that He has not already equipped us for. Now, He may not provide for us in a way that we are expecting or desiring but He always equips us according to His purposes. That includes crises moments that we may never have been in before or have no experience in. We can have faith that where God puts us, He is going to equip us.

Trust. Pause…Listen. Speak.

I learned early that because the Lord knows what I don't, He will know exactly the position I need to take in any situation. All I need to do is seek his input.

Trust. Pause…Listen. Speak.

Anytime I seek the Holy Spirits input, He never lets me down. 20…some years later, especially as a Security Guard in a high school, I cannot imagine not seeking the Holy Spirits guidance.

On a few rare occasions God impressed upon me the role of 'mother' or 'parent'. In every instance the Lord impressed upon me 'mother' it was an occasion where despair was heavy and I was one on one with a youth.

There have been many opportunities to take a parenting stance with a youth and that is no different than any other youth worker who find themselves in a situation where a youth needs a parent more than they need anything else. The longer we work with youth the more we find ourselves in the parental role without any conscious thought. It comes natural.

What was different about these handful of incidents was that each one was a highly charged, very emotional circumstance that was potentially a life altering circumstance.

Each time I felt the Lord pause me…making me aware of needing His guidance.

One of those situations was with a young man who, like many others came from a back ground of gang activity and drugs. I had known him for three years and in that time I watched him throw his education away and bolt headlong down a path to trouble.

Alix was always respectful though. He stayed in the background most the time because at heart, he really did not want the life he had grown up knowing. He wanted more but like many others who grow up knowing gangs and drugs they lack the self -confidence and courage to stand for something different. Alix was a follower. A follower with a kind heart. He was intelligent and very insightful. He had a bit of a temper too.

As Alix spiraled down the drain in drug activity his attendance became more and more sporadic. When he was present he was often under the influence of narcotics. Eventually, due to his activities Alix was suspended from school long term and went into treatment. I did not know if we would see him again.

Several months went by and he returned a very different person. He was clean and with a whole new outlook on life. My teammate and I were delighted by his transformation. He was attending a local church, staying clear of his toxic home environment and away from drugs. Even in the building he was openly walking away from old homies and made it known to all that was not what he was about anymore. He had joy in his heart. It radiated from him; in his laugh, in his smile, how he was with others. God had got a hold of his heart. We talked about his church on a few occasions. He was staying tethered to the one place he knew stability in while the Lord was growing him. I just encouraged him to keep doing what he was doing and told him as often as I could I was proud of him. My teammate, also a Hispanic male, was able to connect with Alix in much needed ways.

The day came where my teammate and I were called in to assist with a drug investigation. At the end of that investigation was a heartache we did not see coming.

Alix, in a split-second moment of what could only have been unconscious habit, took an illegal substance that was passed to him, to hide. Alix was caught in possession. And not just possession but with intent to distribute as well.

Realizing what he had reflexively done Alix even made an attempt to pass it back but the person refused it. Alix was swept up in the search process and it was confiscated from his possession. Honor among homies is one thing that never gets swept away. Even though we knew from the statements of other students what had happened there was nothing that could be done. Alix would not snitch on his old homie.

Alix was in a state of semi shock initially. It had happened so fast but reality kicked in very quickly as law enforcement arrived. My teammate stayed with him through the process as male security. I was close by to relieve my teammate when needed. I have never seen a person so besieged with regret, remorse, and personal devastation to the point of self-hatred as I did in Alix that day. It was heartbreaking to witness. For Alix it was devastating. This 18, year old, young man, with a heart of gold, who had worked so hard to change his life to something different and step into his dream, in a span of three seconds watched it slip away. He cried. Unashamedly begging his mother to forgive him. I will never forget the sound of his desperate pleas of forgiveness from his mother, in the face of her anger.

While Alix's mother met with the police officer and the administrator, my teammate and I stayed with Alix in a separate room. Alix sat in a chair against the wall; hands cuffed behind his back he leaned forward; shoulders slumped and his head hung down. He would not look up to either of us. Tears fell from his eyes to splatter on his knees of his jeans. I stood across the room quietly still so as not to disturb the two men. I watched my teammate sit next to him and encourage him as best he could. Alix needed the words of a grown man.

My job at that point was simply to relieve my teammate when he needed it. A couple times he had to step out. The room was filled with despair, grief and something deeper than regret. It was then I felt the Lord seek to pause me. Turning my mind to Him I began to sense Him speaking.

"Lord, who do I need to be?" and the impression from

the Lord came a little differently this time. "His mother. Love him like your own."

Accepting the charge, I began to process what that meant and look at Alix as my son. I watched those tears leave their darkened spot on his baggy jeans and I asked myself, "If he was MY son, what would I do, right now? What would I say?" Loving them like your own carries its own risks. You have the joy of the mother but you also have the sorrow.

My teammate had to step out leaving me alone with Alix. "Alix," I said as softly. "You are a great young man. NEVER lose sight of that."

Without raising his head, he shook his head briefly as if to deny that then, barely audible he asked me, "Miss, will you give me a drink of water? Please, miss."

"Of course, Alix." I turned and pulled a coffee cup from the cupboard behind me and filled it with water from the tap. As I turned back to walk to him I realized he was not going to be able to hold the cup. He looked up at me and without hesitation positioned himself to sip from the cup as I held it for him.

It was a moment I will never forget. I was instantly reminded of Jesus washing his disciples' feet and the act of humility it was for him to do so. Alix's trust in me wrecked my heart. I have never felt more humbled than I did in that moment by the trust this young man gave me in his hour of despair. It felt like it had the many times I held a sippie cup for my own son as a wee toddler. Alix tilted his head back and I cupped my hand just under his chin to catch any water that slipped from the corners of his mouth and slowly tipped it so he could drink. Three times Alix sipped from the cup and three times I had the honor of serving him as a mother. I felt like I had a vice gripping my chest from emotion. I would not cry for Alix. I would deal with my own emotions later because at that time Alix needed my calmness and reassurance. As he finished sipping I pulled the cup away and stepped back. He brushed his mouth across the front of his shoulder to wipe away the drop that was slipping down his chin.

"You got it?"

"Ya, Miss. Thank you."

I reached out and laid my hand on his shoulder and stood there. He lowered his head again and went quiet. We stayed like that for a brief moment and I could feel his sigh deepen as he calmed down more.

I walked back to the counter to put the cup in the sink and slowed my own heart rate. It was then my teammate walked back in. He updated me on what was happening next and I went on my way leaving the two men. 20 minutes later police escorted Alix, head down as he walked the length of our main hall, hands cuffed behind his back, out of the building with the officer directly at his heals.

Alix has never been back. He would not be allowed

back in any school in the state. It's been years now and periodically his name comes up when we talk about the tragedy of that situation. I saw him once, some time later. I was delighted to see him. He greeted me with a huge smile and hug. Alix was doing ok living with his girlfriend and had a little baby, working full time, going to church and seemed to be doing well. He had continued to stay clean and away from gang activity. He could have given up, but he didn't. Many do. Alix, had locked in and stayed to his course and desire in life: something better than drugs and gangs.

Paul addresses the need to put the past behind us and never look back. Philippians 3:13b,14 *says "...Forgetting what is behind and straining toward what is ahead, I press on toward the goal to win the prize for which God has called me heavenward in Christ Jesus."*

Alix had tasted the hope for which God had called him and he hung on to that hope during one of the most disappointing situations of his life. I have a hope for Alix's future.

The smile and ease on his face told me that which I most wanted to see: the Lord was not done with him yet and Alix's future was bright.

You

I missed you today

The touch

The sigh

The quiet in my soul that is you.

The still of your voice

The warmth of your hug

My name spoken by you alone.

Oh...how I have missed you today

Yet, you were there

Never far; always within reach

Your powerful presence reigning

You

It's always been about you.

My Jesus

BREE

She was ticked. Seething. Like a Screaming Bee fire cracker in its last few seconds before it blows. This short, 15 year old, black haired, Hispanic girl was ready to fight and it did not matter who was in her way. Not even the 6'5" uniformed officer daunted her. She was in the usual attire we saw at that time: black pants (in her case they were tight jeans) and a black tank top. Her hoop earrings were large enough for my entire fist to fit through. Her eyes were outlined with thick, black eye liner that was referred to as "cat eyes". She was solid with muscle and had been around on the streets for years. She knew what was up and was anything but compliant. Every other word was a profainity as she was deliberately obstinate and argumentative.

She hated me.

I sat next to her at the table knowing what she did not and that was I was going to have to search her and her possessions. I was not looking forward to when she was made aware of that. For the moment she was busy cussing out the cop while he took it all in stride. I waited for the Screaming Bee to blow…

I'd had one prior interaction with her and it was an unfortunate introduction. I had broken up a fight between her and another girl already. That did not end well for her. It had been only a couple weeks prior and a situation where she was the new girl and another female had said her name. The fight was on. Coming in as a "Guera" to successfully break it up did not go over well. I knew at the time that she was going to be a female that first impressions would last and since she had, had no other choice but to obey me, she was going to hate me.

Ohhhh…did she hate me.

I watched her and she fairly itched to slap somebody with her rage at being thwarted again from another altercation. (Really, she just wanted to slap me.) She already had a criminal record and was in the legal system. Nothing the cop said made a dent in her demeanor. She did not care who he was, who anybody was, or what they were going to do. It was all old business to her.

An administrator joined us and another female staff person. The time came for me to perform the search and as I expected she was still spewing anger but the process for her was, simply routine. When we were done she sat down, crossed her arms over her chest, leaned back in the chair and spat out expletives to the officer as I reached for her backpack.

It was as I began to go through her things, that I tuned them out and honed in on what was in my hands. There is much to be learned about a person in the belongings they keep with them, either on their person or in their bag. I look through everything. Every pocket, every container, every book, page by page and especially notebooks.

Doodles and drawings and any little hand-written notes are a gold mine to me. As I was moving through my own pattern of searching I was aware that she became more attentive to what I was doing. She began to quiet down and become still...watching me. Her expression of anger eased into concern and then she seemed to be worried. She had completely tuned out the cop as he was talking and instead was intent on me. I was not the only one who noticed her reaction. As I reached for a white, 3 ring binder she finally blew. She was almost hysterical with emotion. She was a mix of anger and fear to the point of tears. This girl did NOT want me looking through the binder. She even tried taking it from me. That is a no-no. She received a very stern *warning* from the police officer and barely contained herself as I opened the notebook.

It was a private journal. I knew immediately, within the first two pages, why she did not want me reading it. It was her heart. It was her outlet. I felt like I had stepped into her most private domain and I had.

It's amazing how fast we are capable of thinking and redirecting. Having a slightly photographic memory, being a speed reader, and experience skimming though countless articles of writing, I knew how to skim her journal without reading her private thoughts. I call it Selective Snooping. I look for key words/phrases to alert me for content that may be of interest. The rest is not relevant and I don't retain the visual.

I was left with the impression of her. The girl had heart and lots of it. There was nothing of relevance to law enforcement nor the school administration but the school administration was very interested in what was in the binder. Busy in conversation between them they also waited for me to hand the binder over to see for themselves. My expression, still intentionally blank, I packed up her belongings. The other adult female in the room made two failed attempts to retrieve it from me.

When it became obvious I was through and they waited for me to call "clear" I took a breath, shoved the binder back in her backpack and made the call.

"She's clear. There is nothing here. The binder is her private writing. She reacted as she did because she did not want her private thoughts read. Again, there is nothing there of interest. No reference to any activity that is of concern or relevant to the investigation."

The cop was satisfied and stood up to prepare to leave but the other woman and admin were not so easily deterred. I expected that and was ready when asked to see the binder.

"Again, I can assure you, there is nothing in her journal relevant to what we have here. It is her private diary."

By bringing out in the open the reason for her agitation, I had put them in a little bit of a tough spot. They would not have reason to further examine what I already had. With that, I handed Bree back her back pack and she snatched it from me with a look of scathing hatred.

I liked her.

I stood there and thought, "Lord, grab hold of this girl. If we can get her on to you she would be unstoppable." It was heartbreaking to see how upset she was by me seeing inside her binder. Thankfully, I had brief moment when the others left the room to speak to Bree privately.

She sat at the table hugging her backpack to her chest, oblivious to the fact that her tank top had slipped off her shoulder and her black eyeliner was now smeared from her tears. She stared at the table; silent.

I sat down slowly next to her in the seat on the right, hoping to perhaps break through. *"Lord, help me reassure her."* She was visibly upset. I chose to speak frankly and matter-of-factly.

"Bree, I know you do not want to hear from me but I want to tell you a few things. I did not read your diary. I understand how important writing can be to someone. It can be deeply personal and I know that. I have my own journals too."

She was not having it. She started to argue and called me a liar and a few other things but I kept talking.

Ignoring her outburst, I spoke directly, "I did not read your thoughts. I was looking for very specific things. Anything else is not of interest to this investigation. I did not see what I was looking for. Your thoughts remain yours. Nobody else will see the diary."

She looked at me with tears in her eyes again and asked, "Really?"

I nodded and reassured her, "Really."

She seemed to be satisfied, to some extent, with my explanation but remained suspicious of me. Time would tell what would become of this young lady.

As the weeks passed by Bree remained extremely volatile. She was every bit a bully. Female students avoided her, the male students were hesitant with the exception of those that she was close to and staff was not a fan. Bree kept us very busy.

Bree's day to day did not improve. She became more antagonistic as the weeks passed. She was a volcano of anger that erupted at any perceived slight. Sometimes there was no slight at all. She just simply wanted to vent her rage. One particular young lady became a target. It quickly became a bullying case that we had to monitor closely. The victim of Bree's targeting struggled for some time and we did our best to keep space between them. Unfortunately, the school could only work within the confines of what transpired on school grounds. What transpired off school grounds would be for the family to address with local law enforcement. As the relationship built between local PD with the victim and legal orders came through, we were able to enforce them on campus.

Ultimately the file of offenses against Bree stacked high enough she went to an alternative school. The consensus was a sigh of relief because she had been wreaking havoc on our campus. It was both a relief and a disappointment to many though. Myself included. I was convinced that Bree raged internally because she ached deeply for the wrongs and injustices in her personal life to be righted. She was fighting a battle in her own home none of us could see and in her war against that, she warred against all.

I liked her.

Bree left and I did not see her for almost a year. I was given a unique opportunity to work at the alternative school for a limited time. Going into that school I was gonna be working with students that had been in my halls but for various reasons were no longer able to stay and enrolled instead, there. I was looking forward to seeing them all again. However, Miss Bree was my wild card. She left my campus still hating me and I had no idea if the passage of time had softened that or intensified it. I was to find out.

I remember the day well. It was mid-morning. The skies were the beautiful blue that I love so much about the area and it was during one of the morning passing periods that I encountered her for the first time in a year.

I was outside, sitting atop one of the park benches, with a half dozen of my past students who had seen me and came over to say "Hi". I was delighted by so many affectionate faces, fist bumps and a few hugs that for a moment I surprised when I turned around and there Bree stood, 3 feet away, looking at me with those intense black eyes of hers.

"Casper..." was all she said. One word. Dead serious. No other emotion.

My reply was one I had thought through in the days before I arrived. I would show her the smile and warmth that I had always felt for her.

"Bree!" I exclaimed. "Hey! So glad to see you!" and I then casually turned slightly away so she could step in and involve herself. It would be her choice but I continued on with visiting happily with the other students.

Bree stood there processing my familiarity and ease with who she then considered her homies. I could tell she was somewhat surprised by the interactions. She didn't say anything at first but, just watched. After a couple minutes she joined a conversation that I was having with two others and when the warning bell rang, I shooed them off to not be late for class. In saying goodbye to them all by name, I called hers as well.

"Later Casper..." was her reply.

I was only there a few days. I discovered Bree had a completely new vibe about her. She was still a firecracker, bold and outspoken but she was tempered. The hard edge of violence was no longer there. Bree had found a home at the alternative school and in doing so it aided her into stepping into her own confidence.

My time there was a joy to me to get to see those students again and how successful they were being in their lives and recovering academic's. It was amazing to see Bree's smile and hear her laugh. I would perch myself atop that park bench in the center of the open, grassy courtyard and the students would inevitably find their way to me to hang out and chat for a few. They would trickle in by groups...cliques... (sometimes by gang affiliation) and shoot the breeze with me. Bree was one of the first. She was a natural born leader.

Over the next few years my ears perked to news of her and what she was doing. She graduated from school and went on into her adult life doing well for herself. I saw her on several more occasions and was always greeted with a smile and even a hug at several events. Bree's kindness was spoken of and I had an occasion to witness it myself in an astonishing way at a major school function a few years after she graduated. So much so I had to step aside for the tears streaming down my face. I could not get the words out of my mouth to tell her how proud of her I was without tearing up again. I never thought to hear her say, "Thank you, Casper." but she spoke it freely.

"Thank you, Casper for putting up with me."

It's been almost three years since that event and I have not seen her since. I may never know what transpired in her life to have caused such an inner turmoil and I will likely not ever know what it took for the turmoil to begin to temper. I cannot even say she came to know Christ cause, I don't know.

What I do know is this: Whether we have knowledge and answers or not, no matter what spews in our face, our calling remains the same: Judge not. Forgive freely. Extend grace, mercy and love. Speak life and encouragement into the darkness. Smile often. Serve endlessly.

Always be ready. In season and out.

"Preach the word; be ready in season and out of season; reprove, rebuke, and exhort, with complete patience and teaching." 2 Timothy 4:2

Wild and free

Moving within His perfect plan
Always loving
with a gentle hand.
Wild and free
His love moves me…
His voice,
His touch,
my mind spins in the dream
Wild, free
Always and forever

            smiling down on me...

MARCO

One morning I arrived to find four people all staring at the camera monitors at the view of our main office. Curious, I took a peek at what they were looking at and began to process the conversation they were having. They were talking about a young male who looked to be about 16 years of age that was standing at the counter talking to a staff person. He looked average enough for what we saw most often. Baggy pants, extra large t-shirt, short cut black hair. He was lean and he struck me as very tired. Even from the camera view I could see that he was tired. The way he stood was very uncertain and hesitant. The conversation about him caught me by huge surprise though. Apparently, they had all worked with this young man before and had some opinions regarding him! There was some serious antagonism to the point of hostility being expressed.

We often share with each other our experiences with students so that was not out of the norm but what was out of the norm was the dislike for this young man. He was an active gang member, an addict, violent, untrustworthy. Someone felt he was a "waste of time and should not be allowed back." I also learned he had just recently been released from juvenile detention where he had been locked up for the last nine months. That caught my attention most. The rest was not anything I would give credence to.

There are several things I have learned in my time working with minors and one of them is this: anytime, anyone is locked up it impacts them in some way and the longer they are locked up, the deeper the impact. For this young man, at his age, to have been in juvie for nine months meant he was in likely for a violent crime and there was no way in the world he was coming out the same young man he went in as. Now, did the time in lock up and getting clean impact him for positive behavior change, I didn't know. But no way was he going to be the kid they had known well over a year prior. Committed to making contact, I left the office to go see if I could intercept this young man before he encountered anyone who had such strong negative opinions of him. He needed the opportunity to have someone get to know him as he was that day; not who he had been, before.

Unfortunately, I did not get to meet him. By the time I got to the office he was already walking out but I did get to be in his presence. Again, I felt his fatigue and hesitancy and just…stuff. Lots of STUFF. In that moment God placed a huge burden on my heart for this young man to "cover him."

The most accurate way to define "Cover" is to "protect".

A command by my Father in heaven would also mean no matter the perceived cost. The interesting thing about the term "cover" is that it involves the use of something else to do the protecting. If I'm told to protect then, I protect. To cover meant that I was to protect by Gods standards even if that were to involve the application of a Biblical standard. In a nation where it is becoming increasingly more frowned upon to apply a Biblical standard in a public school, it gets a little touchy. As always, I would trust that God would take care of me and my family for honoring whatever He put before me.

There have been times where honoring what the Lord placed on me made doing the job a little more complicated. However, every time, God was there in the midst and working for everyone involved. Myself included. And always I had born witness to the miracle of a changed heart and a changed life.

More than once Romans 8:28 has been a life line for me. *"And we know that for those who love God all things work together for good, for those who are called according to his purpose."*

I have never wavered when the Lord placed the word, "Cover" on my heart for someone and with each of those youth I've seen the most difficult and painful circumstances for a youth but I have also seen God work miracles. I had no idea that day this young man, who I would only work with for nine months, would make such a huge impact on my personal ministry.

Knowing then what my role was to be for this young man I turned to go do my "homework." First, I had to find out which administrator he was assigned to and from there start digging and learning about this kids' background. What I learned left me not only thinking, "Holy cow what a mess!!" However, it also had me thinking, "Alright Lord, what have you got in mind cause this young man needs you!"

He had the longest discipline log I'd ever seen for a student. (Still, to this day, I've not seen a longer one.) Pages and pages and pages. And they only spanned 4 years. He had a violent history and a substance abuse problem. He had also been released from the state Juvenile Detention center literally the afternoon prior. Four team members had a meeting specifically about the plan for this young man. That meeting was yet another affirmation that the Lord had his hand on this young, man's life. His three, support staff, like myself, were committed to creating something different for him. All knew him from before he was locked up. All liked him. In that entire day as I asked around they were the only staff I found that had liked him and had had positive interactions with him prior to incarceration. He would be returning to school and going to class the next day. I was assigned to meet him upon arrival and escort him for a tour of the building. It was vitally important to us that he be received with a welcome.

I had also found out he was going to be medicated. I didn't know for what but that was not really relevant to me.

What was relevant to me was the potential for behavioral influence due to the meds. My trip to the nurse was to be met by a still incomplete file. Because he was to be so fresh in the building from lock up there were still more questions than answers. It would seem, we would all be learning in real time.

The following morning, I waited, keeping my ears open to his arrival and when the call came, I was ready. He was more disheveled than the day before but very gracious and kind. He greeted my smile with, a smile. He was also obviously under the influence of something. He was slow… like his mind was in slow motion. I had a hunch what he was on and why but continued on with finishing his re-admittance process. I did not need to explore the mental condition he was in at that point as that would be part of the process anyway.

I learned two very important things about him during the time we toured that morning. There was no deception in him. That was HUGE. By deception I mean he was not a manipulator nor a liar. He was honest. He chose his actions and he would own them. He saw through a filter of accurate reality and he knew right from wrong. Blessedly, he would not excuse or displace blame on others. He was open about the reality of his life.

There is a spirit of deception that we often encounter when we are working with those with behavior issues. I had seen that at work in the many years I had been involved in youth ministry in local church settings and as well in mentoring. Deception and lies are far more pervasive and imbedded in the minds of those where you find the most destructive behaviors. Breaking through the wall of lies, whether it be perceived lies, or spoken lies, is one of the hardest things we encounter. Especially for those whose perception of reality is altered because they perceive reality through a filter of lies.

The second thing I discovered is that he demonstrated Post Incarceration Syndrome (PICS). Not severely but, noticeably in several different behaviors. Having just been released it was not known that this was in play. I first noticed it as we were walking through the main hall. The bell rang for a passing period and the 2000+ students began flooding out of the classrooms. He panicked. Anxiety clearly in his eyes and movements as he spun in a circle looking for a place to escape to.

I felt his fear in a breeze wash over me as I calmly said to him, "Marco, put your back to the wall. It's ok. That's just the passing bell."

Eyes wide he did as I instructed and I stepped in position a foot away and in the direct path of the flood of students filing by creating a break that they all had to walk around. It also put me between him and the mass of people quickly moving within inches of him. He slowly calmed as his initial panic eased.

Once the halls were pretty empty I turned to him and asked, "How long were you isolated?"

He looked at me startled and then realization hit, "I don't know, miss. I lost count of the days."

"Marco, do you understand what just happened?"

"Ya…" and he looked down.

"Come on. Lets' have a chat, you and I." I walked him over to the chairs sitting outside the closest office and he got the 'talk' from me that many get. "I would like to speak openly with you. So long as you're here in my building I promise to do my best to keep you here. I want to see you graduate. That is my agenda: graduation. Everything I do and say to you will be for the purpose of keeping you here in this building. Even when it seems illogical or that I'm against you, I can assure you that I am in your corner. I ask that you trust me. I will always be honest with you even if you don't like it or want to hear it. All I ask of you is 100% honesty and to trust what I tell you to do. I will never judge you. But…BUT…I need you to always be truthful. If I say to you, 'trust me' then I need you to remind yourself of this moment and TRUST me. Even when you don't understand."

There's no sense in giving the "I care about you" and "want you make good choices" lecture. Youth in his circumstances hear that so often their mind shuts off to those well-meaning words and those that give that pep talk are almost immediately put in the "just-like-all-the-other-grown-ups" box. These students need it simple. "I want to keep you in the building" is all that is needed. They don't want to get kicked out of school and that usually is about as far as they are capable of seeing. Stick to what they know. Obviously to be successful with that goal requires heart change and life change and that IS my personal goal but, I don't need to verbalize that. Conversations about heart change and life change happen in teachable moments as circumstances arise. All they need to hear is my agenda aligns with theirs: staying the building and graduate.

So, it began that day. Questions and answers passed between us. Me in my uniform; 5'3", blonde, blue eyed white woman from California who was older than his own mother. Him a 16, year old, heavily tattooed, Hispanic male with a history of violence, drugs, alcoholism and gangs…and a single command from my Father in heaven to "Cover him."

There was so much going on with him. The ground rules for him were that he had to be escorted in the building. His meds were constantly being adjusted because he was having such a hard time adjusting to them. They kept him heavily medicated because of the fear that he would become violent. The problem was the medication he took made him very mentally foggy and he cycled drastically. His down had him asleep in his classes, out so hard that he drooled uncontrollably and could not be woken up. Not to mention he spoke and moved like he was in slow motion. The one perk to being who he was and known with a reputation, nobody had the nerve to bully him in any way. He didn't lose his fights. Because he hit bottom hard he also cycled up hard. His ups had him break dancing in the halls, talking so fast he could make some serious money as an auctioneer and in constant motion. I had to focus hard on following him when he was so animated.

When he plateaued in what I came to recognize as his normal un-influenced state, neither high or low, he was one of the most amazing individuals I have ever known. His IQ was outrageous. Marco's creative talent in drawing, singing, dancing and in music: awesome. The coolest was his natural athletic ability. He was an outstanding wrestler. A natural. His normal temperament was joyful and free spirited. He loved living. Because of his natural joyful, free spirit he was liked and respected by all. Even gang members no matter their affiliation. Outside the building he was known to do business with all. He is the only person I've known to have walked as successfully as he did in all yards no matter the color represented.

Only about two weeks in I was called to pick him up from class and escort him outside to where his mother was waiting for him to deliver his lunch. This was a highly unusual situation. Normal procedure is that a delivery be made to the front office and then the student would pick up from there so for this to happen this way was very unusual. I followed orders, pulled him from class, stepped outside with him where his mother was waiting. I stood about 20 feet away from where he and his mother stood talking in Spanish for several minutes. She had a bag of McDonalds for him. It warmed my heart to see her as she adored her son. That was so apparent. I actually got a little teary-eyed thinking what it was like for her as a mother. I knew enough of her family's circumstance and the criminal history of her oldest sons that the thought of what it was like to have her son home from jail after so long, got me. As a mother of a son, my heart thumped hard for her with compassion. I stood there and reached out to God, *"Lord, help me, help her…what does this family need?"*

Seconds later I received a call on my radio that Marco was needed upstairs. My heart sunk because I did not want to interrupt mother and son. As a Hispanic woman for me, a white woman in authority, to interrupt her with her son could potentially be…not well received. I did not want to earn this mothers dislike. I wanted to be able to connect with her. Sighing, I took a breath and as gently, but with command, as I could, I stated, "Marco, we gotta go." She looked at me and paused…then smiled, kissed him on the cheek and sent him back to me. Words cannot express how relieved I was. As I unlocked the door for our entry I turned and waved back to her mouthing and signing, "Thank you." She nodded in return.

More than once I was called in to pull him from class because he was asleep. It was usually the same class too; English. Marco hated reading. He tried to pass it off that he couldn't read. Even had his teachers convinced he couldn't read. I would go in and quietly tap his shoulder and eventually we would make our way out to the halls. I would either make him walk the halls with me or step outside and do a couple of quick sprints to get his blood flowing again before I returned him to class. Marco always left his books on his desk when we walked out but one day I told him to bring the reading book. Something about snakes and well below his age level. He handed me the book as we walked out of the classroom and I handed it back saying, "No way. YOU read it."

"I can't"

"You can"

"I can't"

"YOU CAN." I stopped walking, crossed my arms over my chest, quirked my eyebrow and scowled at him. "You can. You will. Now read it to me and don't tell me you can't cause you'll tick me off with the lie."

He literally stamped his foot. Like a five-year-old. I started laughing. He started laughing and as we laughed he opened the book and started reading to me about snakes. We walked in the halls for about 15 minutes with him reading to me out loud the children's book. What started out as a frustration for him because I called him out on lying became something amazing. The Holy Spirit joined us... just walking; listening. I could feel the Holy Spirits pleasure hearing Marco read. Marco began to get into the story telling. I just walked beside him and assisted periodically with some pronunciation but mostly just paced him as he read out loud. He was enjoying reading. That day was a turning point for Marco.

As the weeks passed to months he became clearer headed and stable. They leveled out his meds which helped tremendously. He was able to dig in to his academics and his grades rose to all passing. He was wrestling for the schools wrestling team. He was break dancing in the halls, laughing, smiling, making his way through the females. Marco was a flirt and a major chic magnet. More than once I had to send him back to class because he was out walking with a female. There were plenty of de-escalation moments too where security was called in to assist because he was being disruptive either because he was mad or just because he didn't want to work and was busy playing. Usually it was because he was playing but when he was being noncompliant he was a handful. A couple times he was sent home for the day but never more than that.

We had a lot of moments to sit and talk about his history, what put him in jail, the violent streak, the past alcohol abuse and the roll that played in his physical outbursts. I spent a lot of those conversations praying in my mind as he talked, asking the Lord to guide my questions and words. His mother came in regularly. Every time there was an issue, no matter how mild, she had to come in for a meeting with administration. It was during these meetings that I first met Marco's younger, elementary age brothers. She and I would talk briefly afterwards and it was there we began to build a rapport. In her broken English she would ask how he was doing and in my broken Spanish we would somehow, communicate. She would reprimand him, *colorfully,* in Spanish. Sometimes I had to reprimand him and remind him why he was there. However, despite the bumps we all began to witness Marco begin to stabilize and enjoy high school.

Twice, in highly heated moments, I had to call upon him to "trust me". Thankfully he remembered that conversation and did trust me. That good choice kept him from doing something that would have had him out of school permanently and in the follow up conversations we made huge headway in modifying behavior habits.

That was until he began the weekend partying and drinking again. Next: missing school. First, it was a day. Then, it was two days. Eventually he took off and was reported as a run-away. I began getting word of deep alcohol consumption and fighting again. His behavior at school began to get erratic. In our conversations he always admitted it all and acknowledged he was angry at home. The conflicts with his father were becoming increasingly volatile and he was hanging around his "homies" more. Eventually he was removed from the wrestling team. The team of us, his administrator, counselor, nurse, case worker, myself included, watched as Marco slowly began the slide down the drain to alcohol again.

It was crushing. I watched what it did to his mother. Twice I watched as she cried out in fear to the administrator not knowing what to do. She stood in his office with tears rolling down her cheeks. All we could do was stand by as he continued to make ever increasingly bad decisions. Decisions that over winter break ended up putting him back in juvenile detention.

I had said goodbye the Thursday before we went on break and it was to be the last time I saw him as a student. He was not in school the next day. Nor was he in school when we returned from the two-week break. I knew something had happened. Sadly, he had been arrested on another felony charge and was back in lock up where he would be for much longer than 9 months.

It hit us hard. The entire team that had worked with him was devastated. We had all invested not just in Marco but also his mother. We wanted to see Marco and his family step out of their cycles and break free. As a mother it hurt to see Marco's mother hurt. I could not imagine her grief. I still cannot. She made choices in her home to bring some of the decision about but there was never any doubt how much she loved her boys and sought to be a good mother.

At one point, shortly after Marco had been locked up again, she came in still completing his withdrawal from school process. She was a wreck. The little brothers were out of control. The entire household was in chaos. The administrator did his best to console her and, in the end, there was nothing more she could do but, go home. This was the public-school system and it has no authority to law enforcement. While they are partners at times in that law enforcement can dictate what can happens in the schools, the schools do not dictate what happens in law enforcement. As she left that last day I spent some time talking with the little brothers. She hugged me as she left and spoke with her heavy Spanish accent, "Thank you for your help with my boy."

The moments like these are some of the heaviest to get through. The longer we work with people and families that are struggling under the weight of poverty, anger, deception and crime the more we hear the question, "Where is God?!"

The discouragement on this situation was enough that I questioned why I was still working with teenagers. The Lord had told me to "Cover him" and I had covered him to the best of my ability. I took stories of Marco home to my kids and as a family we prayed for him on many occasions.

I remained firm both times I was placed in a position to speak for Marco. I had walked into this case fully confident that we would turn this kids' life around and he would be another radical success story. God impressed upon me to do for Marco as I would my own son. How could it be that it would end this way?!

There were no answers. This was not the first time, by any

means, that we did not see permanent, radical life change. Radical life change does not happen often in the secular world without the influence of God's presence. The separation of church and state makes it very difficult to minister to the heart of the youth by bringing God into the open in the public schools. I do so as much as I can but the reality is there are major obstacles. There is great need for more warriors willing to get dirty in the secular trenches. I had fully anticipated a life change because the Lord told me to, "Cover him."

I cannot speak for anyone else during the time we watched this family go through this but for me personally I had to really press in and hold to faith that even though I could not see the evidence, God was still working in the family. It took me some time to reconcile myself to failure on what my expectations had been and realize that I was not trusting the Lord because of all that I did not know, or see.

Hebrews 11:1 says, *"Faith is the substance of things hoped for; the evidence of things not seen."*

The Lord took this heart struggle of mine and reminded me that what He does he does in His time, in His way and that I had to let go and not feel like I had personally failed.

Some months later, as I sat reading through the book of John I was moved by how comforting Jesus was to his disciples when they experienced the same feelings of dismay and confusion regarding Jesus's revelation to them of his betrayal, death and Peters denial. The scripture says they were "at a loss". I can only imagine their bafflement at what would seem to be illogical and horrifying to them. To credit their faith in their Lord there was not disbelief in Jesus's declarations but primarily shock because it made no sense to them.

We have the benefit of understanding the bigger picture now, on what was happening 2000 years ago but at the time, only Jesus knew. The disciples were operating on blind faith.

As youth workers, as individuals who are working in any area of ministry much of what we do is on blind faith. Some circumstances hit home hard and really challenge us to dig in, to make faith a choice again and act on it. *"Trust the Lord with all your* [our] *heart and lean not on your* [our] *own understanding."* The Proverbs 3:5 scripture is one of my favorites. It's my personal foundation. In circumstances I have faced in my life and in seeing others go through their own, I have stood on that scripture as my rock. There have been times in my life where it became a chant in my head that repeated 100's of times a day. It takes all questions out of my uncertainty. When I commit to trust the Lord without understanding it releases me from the desire to fix or solve something that is out of my hands. My personal confidence needs to remain in Him; not me.

I love that Christ understood the struggle his disciples were facing at accepting what made no sense to them and the fear of upcoming events. He tells them in John 14:1, *"Do not let your hearts be troubled. Trust in God; trust also in me."*

Jesus revealed his and the Fathers heart of compassion

for these men. Even as the time approached for these events to come to pass Jesus never lost sight of being a servant to others. He tells them again in verse 27, *"Peace I leave with you; my peace I give you. I do not give to you as the world gives. Do not let your hearts be troubled and do not be afraid."*

Like the disciples I did not understand what seemed to be illogical. The disciples were asking themselves, "What could possibly be good about Jesus being betrayed and dying?" And I was asking, "What could possibly end in good with Marco seemingly walking away from the progress he had made and making this awful choice?"

The Lord loves us and comforts us even when we cannot perceive what He is doing. With choosing to trust the Lord, no matter the circumstance, comes His Peace and relinquishing the need to understand. When we choose to trust the Lord in all situations, we are choosing to stand on our faith with the expectation of Gods desired outcome coming to fruition thus making way for God to actually increase our faith. The reality is there are times in ministry, in life, where we will not ever understand the "why" of something but we can trust and be recipients of the Lords Peace regardless.

The Lord brought me to another level of trust in Him in the months following Marcos departure and in doing so, came a new measure of peace. Over the years since, I have encountered Marco numerous times and had the wonderful fortune to work with his younger siblings and keep in touch with his mother. I was there as tears of joy streamed down her face as finally, one of her sons graduated high school. Five sons and all but the youngest battled with alcoholism, violence, crime and were involved in gang activity. Only the youngest walked across the graduation platform. Marco is a grown man now, with children of his own, working and doing his best to be a good father and husband. Marco is drug free and lives a life apart from gang activity. Trust the Creator and peace comes...

Battle Ready

The prince of this world now stands condemned
He thinks to chain me; drag me down
No
I stand at the ready
These chains no longer hold me
I am free
I am a child of the One who shattered those chains
I ran
I escaped
The King set me free
Free
Free
Free, to stand at the ready
For whatever may come

Battle ready

THE COLOR GREEN

Kris had the most stunning eyes of any Hispanic female I've ever known. She was beautiful. Even in middle school. Kris was quiet and kept to herself most the time but when she smiled it could light up a room. Kris even had a shy streak that was adorable. Like most from her class she grew up in an environment of gang activity and alcohol.

Kris' high school career started out much the same as it was in middle school. She did a fairly decent job of staying out of trouble despite the fact that most of her female classmates were neck deep in drugs, partying and a few, prostituting. These girls were fighters more than anything else. And not your tug-the-hair-and-scream type of fighting that was for show and most common amongst teen girl fights. When the females in this class went at it, it was gonna get messy. You were gonna have black eyes and bloody clumps of hair being yanked out. Scratches were gouges and they were known to carry weapons. They didn't mess around.

And…I loved working with these girls. Every day it

was something new with them. They had heart. They had passion. They were loyal and they loved. They really did. They were the most stubborn and yet, honest females I've ever had the honor of working with and my green-eyed beauty was right there in the middle of them.

Kris was an artist and exceptionally talented. I was blown away the day I discovered some of her work in one of the high schools display cases. It was the third year I had known Kris and she had kept her little talent quiet from all. I was excited to see what she could do with her gift as was her art teacher.

I was disheartened when I saw Kris' behavior begin to break down. First skipping class, grades dropped to F's, her make up changed to the point she was barely recognizable and she would not respond to any adult in a positive way. While she would not cuss me out neither would she talk openly with me any longer. I could still earn her compliance but as the months progressed that diminished also.

Then, like so many, we began to suspect Kris started coming to school under the influence. It's one thing to suspect a student of being under the influence of a substance; it's another thing to prove it. At that point her behavior reflected minimal engagement with school. The soft spoken, smiling young lady was buried under anger and a chip on her shoulder. Her suspensions racked up and she was out of the building almost as much as she was in between the skipping and suspensions.

At the time we had another group of females making themselves known on the street and in our building. Rivalry had begun and right smack in the middle was: Kris.

It was while I was working at a football game on a Friday night that the entire team was put on alert. There had been a violent altercation at a nearby park with some of our female students. The fight resulted in one of the suspects being taken to the hospital for head trauma. Rumor was the other suspect was: Kris.

Come Monday morning we were expecting the rivalry to continue and word was retaliation was coming between the two groups. We were not disappointed. Within minutes of student's arrival, a second fight broke out involving Kris and another female who was retaliating for Friday's incident. Both girls had come to school prepared. They were dressed the part, lose shorts, fitted tank top, hair tightly braided and gone were the giant hoop earrings. No injuries to either party and as things wound down I sat in an office with Kris. She was completely disengaged. Didn't care what the losses were or the impact to others. She just wanted another go at the females. Kris was angry, hard and brewing hate.

Kris would not sit still but just got up and down from her seat; pacing. I tried to break through the walls to talk with the young lady that I had known but that young lady was hiding under anger and unforgiveness. Of what I did not know. That was to be the last time she was in my building. Kris was suspended and never returned.

It's not easy to have such abrupt endings with students and never find out where they go on in life. I do, however, keep my ear to the ground because fortunately they will usually have friends still in the building that I can ask. In Kris case she dropped off the radar. No one knew where she went.

Till, about a year later, when I got an unexpected assignment. I was assigned temporary duty at the alternative school. I was thrilled at the opportunity to go because at least half of the students there were students that had been removed from my building for one reason or another and it was a great opportunity to see them and work with them again.

It was on the second day I was at the alternative school that I walked into a class and stood at the back scanning the faces looking for the student I needed to pull. Thats when I heard it.

"Casper?" It was said as a whisper but I heard it clearly and turned to see who it was.

At first I did not recognize anyone from the vicinity it came from. There was a young lady smiling at me expectantly but I did not recognize her. I turned back to scanning for the face I had come for but I saw the young ladies' eyes in my mind again. I knew those beautiful eyes. I spun back to look again at the young lady and sure enough it was Kris and she was smiling this huge smile, realizing that I finally recognized her.

"Kris! WOW! Come see me after class!" I whispered a little too loudly but I finally also saw the student I had come looking for.

After that class I was waiting for Kris as she shyly came to me. I could tell she was hesitant and unsure of what my response to her was gonna be. Again, I was stunned at the changes in her appearance and demeanor. I grabbed her by the shoulders and gave her a huge hug. She was wearing a long simple skirt, a very modest shirt with long sleeves and her hair was neatly braided. No jewelry. No make-up. Just her bright, smiling face and beautiful colored eyes. There was no evidence of any gang affiliation in dress or behavior. Just a quietly, modest young lady. We only had a couple of minutes so I walked her to class. It was then I found out that she was in the parenting program. She had a young baby in the nursery and was heading in to cover her time in there.

I got a tour of the parenting facility by Kris and was able to spend several minutes visiting with her and her little one. I was blown away by the transformation I saw. Kris was so wonderfully gentle, softly spoken and peaceful with her baby. Very peaceful.

Over the next couple of days, I was able to chat with her several times. Kris had had her heart turned inside out. She ended up pregnant and that had been a catalyst of change for her. Kris didn't want to feel angry all the time. She didn't want to fight. She didn't want conflict with people. She had not wanted her child anywhere near the life she was participating in and ultimately walked away. Just like that. Took the clothes off. Wiped the makeup off. Said goodbye to her friends and walked away. Kris was living with a new boyfriend who was not father to the child but had taken both of them on as his responsibility.

Kris was surrounded by active gang members every day at the alternative school. They all knew who she was. Rival members and fellow members. The female that she had fought on her last day in my building was there at the school as well. Yet, they all let her be. She kept her head low to not draw too much attention to herself but had made her stand with no compromise despite the heat she took at first. What she didn't know, and I never told her, is that they respected her. I did my asking around and there was a sense of admiration for her. There was no anger in her and she expressed kindness openly to all. She had sought forgiveness from those she had fought and treated all with dignity and respect and in doing so earned a measure of acceptance I had not seen often before. There was, in fact, a sense of protectiveness from many of the other students, for Kris.

I drove home that day reminded how awesome God is and so thankful for seeing her again. The surprise was not over though. The next day when I returned there she surprised me anew. At the end of the day as I was leaving she waved me down from the bus stop where she was waiting with her baby.

I stood there with her and could tell she had something

to say. I played with her little one's hand giving her a few minutes to collect herself to speak what she had on her mind.

Finally, she heaved a sigh, "Casper, I'm sorry for what I did. It was not me. I'm sorry for how I treated you my last day at school. Thank you for all you did for me." She began to get emotional and I politely interrupted her.

"Kris, I am proud of you. You have nothing to apologize to me for. I am so happy to see you loving this little child and away from all that stuff. Just keep doing what you're doing and keep your eyes where they need to be."

I was fortunate in that I was able to have some measure of closure with Kris. More often than not, that is not the case. For anyone who is working with others in a serving capacity, closure is certainly nice, but not necessary. We invest in the lives of others and in doing so we love, with Gods love. At times, we will recall the faces of those we serve for Him and we wonder, "What ever happened to…?" In those moments we have to give that person up again to the Lord. Peace comes in knowing that after all they are His and He knows. Our job is to fulfill our purpose in their lives for the time that He has crossed our paths.

That last day, Kris and I spoke for only another couple of minutes and, I hugged her as I said my last goodbye. I drove home knowing I would not see her again. Young ladies, like Kris, are good for my heart. It's amazing to see such goodness in the restoration of someone's life. It is revitalizing to see how God gets a hold of someone's heart and flips it right side up and witness the resetting of a person's mind and thoughts. A life changed from the heart out is truly one of the most beautiful things I encounter. And not just change in behavior but a change within the heart. The very air around them vibrates differently than it once did. God is so good. Whatever is ahead for Kris in her life one thing I know, she is cradled in the hands of the Lord.

At the Mention of Your Name

At the mention of your name
my heart skips a beat
my pulse races
lips curl into a secret smile
my cheeks flush.

Emmanuel

The love you bestow
on me in private
eclipses
what is seen in public

Yahweh

Merely, at the mention of your name
the unbelievable happens...
stars explode luminescence
the sun radiates with brilliance
Oceans deepen and mountains rise.

Pearline Richardson

Elohim

Mercy, granted so freely
Grace, gifted lovingly
Faith, given eternally
With the mention of your name
the violins strum
the drums pound
the air vibrates
with heavens glorious sound.

Adonai

All at the mention of your name
the eagle soars higher
like the lover who makes
my heart softens
so, you are to me
my Yeshua

Always, you are my love
Forever, Ill sing your praise

Simply, at the mention of your name.

BIG THINGS IN
LITTLE PACKAGES

I'll never forget the day I saw her. She was adorable. She was an itty-bitty, tiny girl with a swagger that told everyone she ruled her world. She was feisty as all get out. There are no other words to describe her. She was loud. She was bold. She would not accept nonsense from anyone. She laughed with everything she had and she was respected.

Granted she was also bullied but it never made a difference. She stood up to anyone and profanely would tell them to "FLIP Off!" It didn't matter if it was an adult either. If someone was so bold as to harass her about her size she gave them a piece of her mind and if it was one her siblings or cousins giving her grief, her fists gave them a licking right along with her sassy mouth. Her siblings were harsh at times with her but more than once we had to step in to cool an older brother down because someone was harassing her. Her siblings would tolerate no one bullying her. She never needed their help though and would actually get just as angry at their interference. She had zero hesitation to take anyone on. No fear.

She was the next best thing to brownies in my opinion. In our whole teams' opinion actually. She was refreshing.

She was also from a family with whom I had worked with all but one of her older siblings. She was one of 11 children in the family; #6 in the lineup and all were born into severe poverty. They all lived in a tiny trailer. Not one of them, nor their parents had graduated high school. In fact, no one in her family, extended or otherwise, had. Her parents never went past middle school and only one of her older siblings made it to a senior in high school. However, much to my disappointment that ended in a drop out status as well.

This little pipsqueak swore from day one she would be the first to graduate. Her freshman year she was in a few fights. She was little with a big attitude and made it a point to establish her ground. She did well. Her sophomore year we saw no altercations but she was a busy bee with skipping school and just general sassiness. She was still awesome.

I checked in with her often to nudge her in the direction of graduation. Ok, I nudged…a lot. I told her frequently as did several, "You're gonna break the cycle and pave the way for those coming in under you. Its gonna happen! You're gonna be the one to show your little brothers how it's done."

Every chance I had I told her, "I am so proud of you.

Stick with this!" Always reminding myself that words have the power to heal, to sooth and encourage.

"Death and life are in the power of the tongue, and those who love it will eat its fruits." Proverbs 18:21

Paul was wise when he spoke so aptly in Ephesians, 4:26 *"Let no corrupting talk come out of your mouths, but only such as is good for building up, as fits the occasion, that it may give grace to those who hear."*

Coming from a man who had his life turned upside down when the Lord confronted him for his own behavior and persecutions of Jews, Paul was more than qualified to give us instruction on how the Lord expects us to speak.

Again, in Colossians he says, *"But now you must put them all away: anger, wrath, malice, slander, and obscene talk from your mouth."*

Not only are we given clear direction about how not to speak but we are given instruction about to build each other up.

"Gracious words are like a honeycomb, sweetness to the soul and health to the body." Proverbs 16:24

"Let the words of my mouth and the meditation of my heart be acceptable in your sight, O Lord, my rock and my redeemer." Psalm 19:14

"Let your speech always be gracious, seasoned with salt, so that you may know how you ought to answer each person." Colossians 4:6

Because I know how vitally important it is for others to hear encouraging words it is the biggest part of what drives me in my job and who I am as a person. Sadly, I do not always succeed. Sometimes, I have to be very intentional about speaking in kindness. In a world so full of sarcasm and negativity we must bring the Lords grace in word, to those who need to hear it. Not just because we are given instruction how we are to speak but because of how we are to love. Let His love flow in our speech. His children need it. Desperately.

"The good person out of the good treasure of his heart produces good, and the evil person out of his evil treasure produces evil, for out of the abundance of the heart his mouth speaks" Luke 6:45

This young ones biggest obstacle to overcome was a spirit of complacency that permeated within her family structure. Her older siblings were gang affiliated and there was a history of drug activity in the family; not to mention physical abuse within the home. We were all pulling for this girl. The odds were severely stacked against her but she kept at it with a solid head on her shoulders. Despite the constant discouragement and criticism, she faced, she kept plugging away at high school.

There was no major catastrophe in her life to derail her. Even if there had been a major crisis it would not have budged her from her goal. What corroded at the graduation target was the complacency and the discouragement that surrounded her. Her junior year came and went and at the start of her senior year came the announcement that she would not be graduating. Too many unpassed and unrecovered required classes in her freshman and sophomore years resulted in not meeting graduation requirements.

For the first time I was seriously concerned that she might drop out. She was crushed. Her usual peppy self was subdued and her vibrancy was gone.

Personal discouragement is a powerful thing. It's a huge obstacle to face. You've got a student facing the ramifications of their own actions. Then, reality sets in that nothing is going to change and they will not graduate on time. At that point they remember well how many times they were encouraged to make better choices.

Students that don't graduate progress through the same cycle of emotions. At the end they face a decision: to continue in school or drop out. Every single student who fails to graduate on time will have to make that decision. How do you see them through that process? It's rough. Any pressure coming from parents plays a pivotal part in their final decision. If there is encouragement at home, they continue on. If there is anger and criticism at home: rarely do they continue.

I don't know what my wee, pipsqueak got at home. I never asked. It didn't matter what others told her. What mattered was what did she want and that is what I tapped into. Yes, I wanted her to continue but even that was not relevant. She needed to step up and stand on her own feet. I knew in her heart she wanted to continue and that was what I focused on. I spoke to her on the assumption that she would. I assumed she would and I let her know it and I encouraged her in that every time I saw her. In the last semester of her senior year it was to my delight I saw her head tilt with more self-assurance and she owned the halls once again. She would return in the fall and graduate in winter. She embraced it and that became her new goal.

She walked with confidence and took a role of leading the underclassmen who were spending too much time skipping and not focusing on grades. Numerous times I came across her giving some poor freshman, who usually stood well above her, a heated shout of, "stop being a brat and go to class!"

The Fall year began and Pipsqueak was present as was a new sibling. It was a joy to see her younger sibling walk the line. A shy, young man, he kept his head low, out of trouble and while a struggling student academically, he had no other focus. He spoke little but was busy as a student. I kept my eyes open for him and my ears to the ground for anything to be of concerned activity. A quiet, shy young man who would remain in special education classes but with a kind heart, I did not see him much. He spoke little but was busy doing as a student should do. I kept my eyes open for him and my ears to the ground for anything to be a concern for.

Finally, the announcement came for the winter

graduation ceremony. It was a wonderful ceremony. Very short with only a half dozen mid-year graduates. Her whole family attended the small ceremony. Several staff, including my teammates and I attended as well. Everyone looked on with pride as, she smiling radiantly, received her diploma. I watched the pride in her siblings faces, and that of her parents, as many tears flowed. It's amazing what happens in a family unit when there is a "first to graduate." It is one of the coolest things to watch unfold.

When the crowd around her cleared some, I made my way to congratulate her. I was greeted by the smiles and fist bumps of her older siblings. The look of recognition in her mother's eye as our eyes met will stay with me. I had seen her children through their middle school years and the years of high school. The times when they were in trouble at school my face was usually around.

"Gracias…" she said through glassy eyes with tears.

"De 'nada." I replied as I smiled with tears stinging my own. "We have one more and we will get him through."

She nodded and I discretely left the excited gathering family. It was good. I was struck anew at how good God is and how fortunate I am at times to bear witness to the success's others fight to reach. This was one of those moments. I knew this triumph would be a launching pad for more to come.

Four months later I was called to a classroom that reportedly had no teacher. I arrived to find it was a Special

Education class. Several were behavior students therefore, we were on familiar terms as is normal for my job. However, one of the students was Pipsqueaks little brother. While not a behavior student he was still SPED. Surprisingly, the class was well behaved while I was in the back making the needed phone calls. It was while I was on hold contacting the office regarding the arrival of the substitute teacher that I was pleasantly surprised by what I watched happen.

He got up out of his seat, walked to the front white board where the binders were stored and passed them out, softly giving instructions for what they needed to do. His classmates, who were notorious for being unruly and disrespectful, listened to his every word and followed his direction. He took ownership of his classmates and led. It was amazing to watch! I knew right then that the ripple effect of his sisters' successful graduation was already impacting her family.

Every word of encouragement matters'…

"A gentle tongue is a tree of life…" Proverbs 15:4a

HIGHLIGHTER HEAVEN

In 1963 Carter's Ink Company brilliantly brainchilded the: highlighter. Chubby and thin they come in a small variety of fluorescent colors. Where would we be without them? Every college student has them today like they have their sugar fix next to them in the wee morning hours studying. High school students have them as well as middle school students. We have them in our office drawers. I have 2 next to my laptop even as I write this. In all the personal possessions I have searched I can pretty much tell you who is going to have pencil pouches full of these brightly hued focusing tools.

And that's what they are: focusing tools.

We use these wonderful resources to draw our eyes to that which we desire most, easiest and quickest to recall. We want to retain and recall the meat and richest part of what we are studying. My 23-year-old study Bible is full of pink highlights. The book I am currently reading about emotions has its smattering of yellow highlights.

Those pieces of text are what I want to see when I look at that page again. I want my eyes to be drawn to those words so, I highlight them. I let my eyes read, linger and smile on those words. Sometimes I avert my eyes to all other words altogether. Other times they be in my peripheral vision only providing perspective to what I am reading.

As youth workers we are often in a position to see all kinds of behaviors. In my job I am called in to address the disruptive, and even destructive, behaviors of students. It can be difficult at times to keep the focus on positive behaviors when you are working with an individual who doesn't see anything positive about themselves or their life and they behave as such. We need to be the first to see beyond their destructive behaviors to the beauty that God created within them. Every person has been lovingly and intentionally created by the God of all creation. He did so with purpose and design. The precious gold that is within every person needs to be carefully cultivated and nurtured so that it can grow, mature and flourish. As it does so, there is a natural process of problem behaviors becoming corrected.

We have to see in others what they don't see in themselves and reflect it. Call it out. Put it in words to them. When they have no kind words: we use kind words. When they have an unforgiving heart; we demonstrate forgiveness in our own. When they have no smile; we show them a genuine smile.

They need to be acknowledged with respect. They need

to know there is more, so much more, for them than what they have known. We need to be the first to say, "Hey! How are you today?" Then, we need to give them our undivided attention and let them hear us say, "Hey, I'm glad you're here today."

We have others, their positive attributes. Tell them. Find a compliment. Look for the attribute that needs to be highlighted, call it out and keep doing so over and over again. Then, look for more attributes to highlight. Paul says in Philippians 2:3 *"Do nothing from rivalry or conceit, but in humility count others more significant than yourselves."*

This comes from a posture of humility; yielding to what the Holy Spirit says about someone and seeing beyond the behavior that is presenting itself in front of you.

It is not always easy to do because sometimes the situation, or the person, in front of you is not very…pleasant. To say the least. I know that there are times when I fail at this and I let a situation push my buttons.

One time I was called in to search a young female who was known for having a temper. She was hostile and hateful from the second I walked in the door. In fact, she was already in that state of mind before my arrival. I just joined the mix as my job dictated. I don't typically take offense to the verbal barrage of angry abuse that comes my way from a teenager as I know full well it has nothing to do with me. I just happened to be the one that gets paid to respond to situations that are already transpiring.

Initially I was cool and began to work towards de-escalating her anger. We did fine and I was pleased she was following my lead in calming down.

Right up until I began to prepare her for my search. At that point she escalated right back up the fire pole to hate level 8. Apparently, this was not to remain one of those emotionally unaffected days for me. 5 minutes after listening to her profane, racist explosions, "I hate white people and I hate all you, white chics..." then it started coming in Spanish too.

This verbal barrage was coming in multiple languages and unfortunately, I understood it all. Spoken in English a youth can unload on me all they want and it might as well be water on a duck. However, as soon as it starts in a different language that's when I, personally, have to bite down a wee bit on my pride. Somehow, when being verbally spit on in a language other than English, I struggle. This young lady was on fire. I had no idea what set her off initially or the situation that she was entangled in but I was now her rage target...in Spanish. However, I still kept my mouth shut.

Then, she started trashing on me to another staff person and he joined her in speaking in the language. She threw every foul thing you could think of at me.

10 minutes later I'd had enough...peeved I spoke up. Typically, I would have remained quiet and not spoken. Eventually they run out of steam when they have no one talking to them to respond to but, sadly I became offended

and broke my silence. I think I said something to the effect of, "If you change your tone just enough you could start singing and make a pretty good song with that language you have. If you want we could sing in harmony. We could tag team it. You sing your 'Go flipity-flip-flip yourselves' and Ill sing my 'No thank you's'"

The sarcasm was not one of my finer moments and did not go over well. An hour later after she spewed rage and threats at 5 other staff including 2 other security specialists, she finally calmed down.

Unbelievably, she came looking for me to apologize to before she left campus.

I was stunned. I did not see that apology coming. I've had many kids over the years come to me and apologize for how they have treated me in their anger at other things but this apology was a surprise. I had already felt convicted of allowing myself to have become offended and my response to her and was kicking myself over it. I was very thankful for the opportunity to speak to her again but I was not expecting an apology from her. The Lord humbled me further in that moment.

All I could think to say was, "Thank you for that but there is no need to apologize to me. I should not have let it get to me like I did and I apologize to YOU. You deserve better from me and I am sorry".

She said thank you and was on her way. I was surprised

to find out later that she did not apologize to anyone else. She had specifically only come looking for me.

More than once over the years I have had a student say that for me to give a harsh response or get angry with them at anything is what told them they were out of control. Something about my reprimand to my students gives them pause. I have asked myself, "What is it about me that convicts them of their behavior?" I have sought to understand what brought the apology and I asked them. Every time the response has been essentially the same: I spoke to them respectfully or kindly no matter how they spoke to me.

We know that Gods kindness leads us to repentance (Rom 2:4) and I have seen this principle play out. Our own kindness is not our own. Anything good in me is not of me but rather that of my Father. Any smile in my countenance is not of me but rather that of the Father. Any light in my eye is not of me but also that of the Father. Any wise words or caring heart is not of me but rather that of the Father. As the Holy Spirit is in me so He can shine out to others. All things good and holy come from the Father and it's my commission to let Him impact me in a situation in the hope and fulfillment of the promise that He will do the work needed.

James 1:17 says is clearly, *"Every good thing given and every perfect gift is from above, coming down from the Father of lights, with whom there is no variation or shifting shadow."*

We also know that a gentle answer turns away wrath. (Pro 15:1) Kindness, shown to others when they are being anything but pleasant, goes a long way to bringing reconciliation and a self-awareness within themselves.

So how, as in this case when I obviously lost objectivity, is it that something clicked in her head? Because that's who God IS and that is what He does. He's cool like that. The tenderhearted Father can take our mess ups and create something with them that we would not have been able to on our own.

What do you do when God moves in a situation in an awesome way that only He can and He does it with your mess? Praise Him for being who He is that he makes beauty from ashes.

I don't know what happened in her heart, to go from being angry and full of rage, to apologetic and kind when she came looking for me an hour later. No one can know fully but I do know that only God can do that.

Our last exchange lasted only about 60 seconds but that was long enough to remind me of the importance of being deliberate to call out the good and beautiful in the students I work with and in society as a whole. I made a mental note to be on the lookout for this young lady and whenever I saw her make an opportunity to have a positive exchange with her. Every opportunity to reinforce a good behavior, kind word or declare good in their lives is an opportunity to highlight that which the Lord has placed in their heart and lives.

DIVINE ENCOUNTERS

It was an early Fall morning; the sun was bright and warm as it shone through the tall windows of the gym entry way. I had finished up my hall rounds within the massive building and decided to pause at a table outside the bathrooms. I noticed our day custodian came out the boy's restroom and as she did so she locked the door so no one could enter. I didn't think much about it other than note that that was the first time I had seen that bathroom locked during the course of a school day. I processed it because with it locked that would mean that all of the classes in that area would have to send their students to another section of the facility if they needed to use the restroom. Which meant: more foot traffic through that area. A few minutes later a young male, wearing his hoodie up over his ducked head and his shoulders hunched came around the corner headed to the boy's restroom.

As he approached I quietly told him, "Hey…it's locked. You're going to need to head to another restroom."

It was then I got a glimpse of his face. He was crying. His cheeks were flushed and wet with tears. He was probably about 16 years old, stood 5'8" ish, lean frame, blue eyes, sandy brown hair that was a bit shaggy and flipped up at the ends.

It was like looking at my own son. Same build. Same hair. Same posture and the way he moved told me he was a runner and a soccer player also like my son. My heart sunk.

My son, 18 years old at the time, had been battling with some things in his personal life that was creating an inner turmoil of anger and sadness. He and I, for the first time were battling each other in our relationship. It was tearing me up personally and I know it was affecting him deeply.

How does a mother describe a son? I adore him. I have two daughters and they are very different and I adore them too but a son…is a son. I knew what he was going to look like when I was six months pregnant. I had a dream where I was holding him as a baby and in the dream, he wore blue denim Osh Kosh B Gosh overalls. I could see his little face, blue eyes and his full lips. He was perfect. Preciously perfect. I felt his character in my dream and I woke with the impression of two things: quietness and boldness. I knew then the name his father and I chose for him was not something we chose, but instead was laid on our hearts. Caleb was just who he already was and would be. I knew who my children were before they were born but none so vividly as my son, Caleb.

This particular day happened a few days after my son and I had had a huge argument. It had become volatile, harsh and flat out ugly. As the parent I had failed to be the loving mother I should have been no matter what I faced in him. As a family we had walked a dark path in our home a year prior and my son was having a difficult time with events. He hurt and he was angry and at 18 years old he and I seemed to be on opposite side of a wall at times.

This young man with tear tracks had the same look about him that said the world was heavy on his shoulders. My heart clenched with a desire to help him.

"Hey…come here for a second." I beckoned softly. He made his way to the table with his head down and I simply asked him, "You ok?"

"Ya miss…" Tension exuded from him as he pursed his lips and held back tears.

"Hmm…I can see differently. Can I do something for you? I can give you a quiet moment if you need one." He nodded and I could tell he was struggling not knowing if he should speak or not. After a while you get to recognize keenly when someone is debating on if they should speak. Gently I continued, "I'm sorry for whatever is going on. I understand wanting to talk and yet, not. I can listen if you just need a minute to get some stuff off your chest or if you just need time to clear your head you can hang here with me. You'll be fine here."

He scrubbed his face with his hands and composed himself a bit, "Miss, can I talk to you?"

"Of course." I smiled knowing that whatever he was carrying he was going to lay down. I kept my face pleasantly objective, my voice clear but gentle and waited patiently. Understanding the language of teenagers, in need of a listening ear, is about being patient, letting them lead and never pushing. As I waited for him to find his words I said a silent prayer, "Lord, you know what is going on. I do not. I need your wisdom please. Direct me. Help me…"

I knew this was not going to be easy for me personally because there was something about this young man that tugged on my "mother's" heart. I had no idea just how much this interaction was about to move me.

It was surreal. The ray of the sun shining in the window cast its light and warmth across the table and created a glow in the area that brought my senses wide awake and I could feel the Holy Spirit close. I could sense the Holy Spirits gentleness and I knew then, whatever was ahead would be meaningful. I felt the impression of TRUST from the Holy Spirit. It was not a reminder to me to trust Him but rather He touched on the place in me that does trust Him. More like He activated what already lived within me and I felt it. I trust the Lord with all my heart and lean not on my own understanding. That is my lifeline and I pressed into that trust with a silent plea for guidance for myself.

What followed was an amazing account of a young man's

life who in the last four months was an astonishingly exact replica of my own sons. Our families events were identical. I was blown away. Beginning with dealing with an affair breaking up his parents relationship, massive home repair work due to unexpected damage, loss of transportation, loss of family income, sibling crises and an anxiety riddled home resulting. The young man was, in fact, carrying the weight on his shoulders as the only male remaining in his house. His mother and sisters were doing their best to keep it together but as a male he felt the weight in a way that only males do: to be strong and carry the responsibility of fixing it all. All that and he was still hurting from his own crushing disappointment and afraid because he could not help his mother or sisters deal with their fears.

I struggled in listening to him. Twice, I teared up and turned away briefly. The Lord had brought me to a unique place to hear my own sons' heart from an unexpected source: the words of this young student standing at the table with me. It was a gift to a mother. The Lord was giving me the gift of perspective; how to better discern how these two young men were experiencing their pain. As such, revealing to me how to best serve them. I began to understand more of what my son needed from me. Most importantly, how to begin praying.

As this young man stood in front of me, I leaned into the Holy Spirit to help set my own emotions aside and serve him how the Lord directed me to. He needed a mother he could be vulnerable with, get personal encouragement from and a little bit of insight. I recognized that he was in a position of trying to be "the man" for his family. My kids, and I, had walked this path in our home too. While we were, in part, still healing we had come far and had experienced restoration through the process. He needed reassurance that his family would as well.

I eventually asked his permission to speak freely. Speaking freely as myself is sometimes different from my role in my job. It never contradicts my responsibility in my job but it can come in addition to my job on occasion when I feel someone may want to hear from me personally. Permission though is something I require. I am open in my faith and I will share it with anyone, including my students but only with permission to speak freely.

"I'd like to speak with you about a few things you shared. Is it ok with you if I speak freely?" And as I asked that I took my right hand and I covered the title on my uniform. He noticed it and nodded.

I went on, "I'd like to talk to you as just me. Not as security. If you'd rather not, I get it." I smiled again so he would know it was ok to say, "No" and again he nodded and said, "It's fine. Go ahead."

I took a deep breath, another quick, silent prayer for guidance and dove in the deep end. "I think there is reason we are here today. Thank you for sharing with me what you're going through in your family. I am so very sorry for all the hurt and disappointment for everyone. I understand in many ways what your house is going though…"

I shared with him as the Holy Spirit led me to. Again, I had to step aside at one point with my own tears. In sharing with him about my own son was where the difficulty lied. However, there was great comfort to him in hearing how another young man had walked the path he was on and struggled with some of the same feelings he did. It calmed him some. Being real with him about anger was the most difficult but the Lord kept pressing me on to emphasize the importance of releasing the anger and forgiving.

I tread carefully when speaking as a mother who has walked this path. The hardest aspect for me personally had been trying to support my own kids in their fears and hurts when I was also broken from my own. One of the worst things for a parent to experience is the feeling of inadequacy to their kids needs and seeing them hurt emotionally and helpless to stop it.

This young man helped me serve my son and opened my eyes to some things I needed to see. The same held true for him. There was a deeper understanding and strength when he walked away from me because the Lord had worked in him encouragement. It was such an honor to see him walk away with a lite step, shoulders up and straight, hood down on his back and a small smile on his face knowing these things would pass and he was not alone.

I stayed there at that table for a while after he returned

to class and just was in awe of how amazing God is. Only He could have pulled that off. The Father of all that is good knows our needs and loves to serve us with provision. Sometimes that provision is in encouragement and understanding. Being willing to share what lies on our hearts, and the battles we have already fought and won, can be a game changer of encouragement to others. I don't know who walked away feeling more encouraged; that young man or myself but I do know that the hope sparked from a shared testimony connects the Lords believers and can move mountains.

God is good.

ADDICTION

I despise addiction. I hate seeing what it does to people. Addiction is an insidious evil. It has no age preference; no racial discrimination; no gender partiality. It targets anyone who is breathing. It blindsides its victims and leaves them buried under the cloak of lies, condemnation, shame and self-destruction.

Heartbreakingly, addiction comes in many forms and not just substance abuse. The first things that most often come to mind for a substance addiction is drugs or alcohol. However, addiction really can include any behavior or substance. Anything from candy, pencil shavings, and energy drinks to name just a few.

Then, there is the behavioral side of addictions like sexual addiction. That can include sex, pornography and several other mediums that are now prevalent due to modern technology. Sadly, there is such a deep need for affirmation, on some level, the youth are seeking it from any source. Sexting and picture swapping, on-line sex and more. As much as I wish I could say I do not see these behaviors often, I can't.

So often when a person begins walking in the path of these behaviors it is because they are seeking to fill a void, or hurt, from a missing or painful relationship. There is a lack somewhere in their life and most often that lack is in relationships with others. Especially vulnerable youth seem to be those with significant parental relationship issues.

Many addicts fall in the cracks. Witnessing anyone having their butt kicked by addiction; seeing them transform before our eyes; the faded, faraway look; hearing the lies that they believe is a nightmare to all who love them. No one wants that.

While the hurting addict seeks relief the addiction itself seems to seek one thing: to kill its victim. First by killing the human spirit with shame and condemnation. Then, by killing relationships and isolating the victim. Lastly, by taking the life of the addict. Literally.

I hate it.

Many years ago, early in my career I was working with a small church in Oregon. I was about 19 years old and there was a young teen we saw regularly. I knew a little of his background and it was a broken one. Sadly, he was unable to connect with his guardian. He was probably 14 at the time, a little overweight, long hair that hung to his shoulders, always wore black and loved his metal music. He was a sweet young man; full of laughter and sass and a wonderful future.

As the months passed we saw him less and less. A couple times I was present when there was a home visit to check on him and each time he seemed more distant than the last time. He lingered in my mind and I wondered how he was fairing. Periodically, I would ask and the usual report was not positive. Eventually there was no report at all. No more contact was attempted at that point. As young as I was, and only in a position as a volunteer, I didn't know what, if anything to do. I did not understand why I seemed to encounter an attitude of "Oh well..." with regards to this young man. I didn't know what to do.

Two years later, at a high school graduation, I saw him one more time and it was the last time I ever saw him. He was taller, buzzed hair, skinny, wearing pink and white stripped, stretch pants and a white shirt. His mannerisms were completely different; feminine. His personality was totally different. On his face were faint sores. I was so taken aback at what I faced that I didn't believe who I was told he was. The transformation was profound. I found out that night that his life was living on the streets as a male prostitute and he was an addict. I was stunned and crushed. Once again, as I spoke to the adult leaders who had worked with him I encountered grief, but there was also the tale-tell shrugging of shoulders and the look of, "Oh well...we tried".

Everyone had done all they *knew* to do. I worked with good people who genuinely loved on troubled, at risk, youth. There were as grieved as I had been at the change in this young man. However, I was never at ease with the response that specific young man received. I never forgot him. We moved to another state shortly thereafter and I never again got an update on him but his effect on me was deep and lasting and impacted every contact with an addict thereafter. He became my filter for how vital it is to *connect* with an addict.

I learned from him that every contact is, in fact, not just about that one moment, but about that moment and *every* moment to come after. I learned that how you walk away from a contact is how you will approach them the next time. Moments with an open heart of compassion open avenues and that is the heart of connection. That is the heart of the Lord.

When we are able to successfully connect with an addict (any hurting person) we can become the conduit by which the Holy Spirit can speak to them in a new way. We can be the tangible evidence of the Father loving on them in a moment of kindness. We can draw them in or repel them. The Father draws them in. The world repels. The world is big but our loving Father is bigger.

Those were not easy lessons to learn but I am so thankful to have learned them early on. They changed ME and forever how I have worked with addicts. In 27 years, the precious faces who lost the battle to addiction are faces that I will never forget. Many are sadly lost in the cracks because an addict is not able to maintain relationships and end up disappearing. All of them have attendance issues in school which makes the process of getting them help all the more difficult. When the addiction is to an illegal substance then, when they are caught under the influence or in possession those discipline logs begin lengthening. Not to mention the criminal aspect that also plays a part. Addiction is a life consuming.

However, I have been privileged to witness those who have overcome addiction. It is one of the sweetest processes to see happen. It's like watching a toddler learning to walk; a fragile, hesitant process full of trepidation and wonder at the same time. There are falls along the way but if there is conviction and grace they rise again and keep going. It's wonderful. To see them breathe and look out at the world with eyes wide open in amazement is not something to be forgotten. It's joyous. They radiate.

One such success was young lady named Aubrey. She was 15 at the time. Skinny. The first time I met her she had the stink of poverty and drugs about her from long periods of un-washing and as normal, avoided eye contact. Aubrey's poison was Meth. She was a liar and cheat and talked non-stop with her fantastical stories. Her beautiful pale face was tainted by meth sores as were her arms.

I saw her often and was always on the lookout for her when I didn't see her which usually meant she was locked up. Time and time again when I reached out to contact her she was high. Time and time again, it was difficult to communicate with her because her reality was so far not… reality. She was already in the system so my job was pretty simple: keep a look out and keep others on notice of her where a-bouts and condition. Whenever possible I spoke at length with her and rarely got past the fantasy she lived in. Eventually Aubrey began dating a guy, a couple years older than her. Unfortunately, he had a violent temper. Things continued to spiral out of control for Aubrey as both her and her boyfriend became so consumed by meth I hardly recognized them any longer.

Then, as many do, she disappeared. Not a word of her from any contact that I had.

Till, one day about 2 years after I last saw her, I walked into one of the upscale restaurants not far from the town I lived in and there she was: the hostess and radiantly beautiful.

I stood there with my mouth hanging open, gaping at her. She was in glowing health, vibrant with bright eyes and laughter that echoed in the waiting area. She radiated happiness and freedom. There was nothing left of her that would indicate she had been wrapped up in meth 2 years prior. Not even scars on her skin. She absolutely glowed.

It brought tears to my eyes. Aubrey greeted me with a huge smile and a quick hug as I tried to recover my composure and wipe the tears away. It was a delight to grab a few moments to talk with her privately. We did not have much time that night but a few months later I returned and she was working that night as well. We were able to speak more at length. Her path after I had seen her had indeed been a dark one. After reaching a point of desolation in the abusive relationship and buried in self-loathing she began the process of finally coming clean and staying clean. Aubrey had severed all relationships in the process starting with her boyfriend. Aubrey also walked away from her family and her friends. She moved out of town, got a job and continued climbing out of the hole. Aubrey was healthy, strong and very much of sound mind. She was bold about her past, coming clean, staying clean, keeping toxins out of her life and stepping out to be an encouragement to others.

To this day, many years later, Aubrey is still clean and is a voice of hope to others to come clean.

Father,
our hearts sing with joy
in the promise of broken addiction.
Nothing is greater than you.
Let nothing separate us from you.
We were made to be addicted to only one thing
and that is
You.
We can never have enough
Grace and Mercy.
We can never have enough of
Your faithfulness and goodness.
We need more of You, Lord.
Nothing else but You.

Amen

FROM THE END TO
THE BEGINNING

Nearly 15 years ago, as I sat at the computer, a skeleton of an idea that had been floating around in my head for years began to take form. Youth ministry is its very own unique ministry and those in it for the long term are most definitely their own breed. I have always greatly respected them and their commitment to youth. Youth workers are often bold, direct and passionately love youth.

Many youth workers are just big kids at heart in one way or another and well, that is an essential quality. To effectively work with youth, having the stamina to be able to play, laugh, cry, and most importantly, love with an endless patience is vital. We gotta be willing to meet them where they are. I'm not saying go out and jump on a skate board (cause if you're like me that would be a bad plan and could potentially involve earning a bunch of unplanned bruises) but just being willing to go out and join them curbside makes all the difference.

The Lord has had to challenge me in many areas over the years; even hunker down hard a time or two on my attitude. By the time I wrote an outline for Radical Transformations I had been working with youth for 10 years and was on staff as a Children's Director overseeing a thriving children's ministry in a small church in California. I loved children's ministry. I was continuing to mentor teens on a volunteer basis in addition to assisting my husband in his youth ministry as needed.

I knew one day I would be working on that book. I wrote a few outlines and intros to a couple of the chapters and saved it.

It sat. For another 10 years. Untouched.

Writing a book had floated around in the back of my mind but never grabbing hold. My marriage fractured in a dark place of my life as I took my eyes off the Lord. We moved to Washington where I became a single mother to 3 beautiful children and my husband and I, after 16 years of marriage, navigated through divorce.

In the early years following my divorce, as I wondered in my walk with the Lord, I was taken back to my promise I made as a young teen. I had vowed a life of standing in the gap, and for those in need.

At 38 years old I began to realize there was unhealed pain from my childhood that I was carrying that needed to be given to the Lord to heal. I spent several years searching the wrong places for answers to quiet the noise in my heart. I never stopped loving the Lord and searching for Him but I was wandering. From there I began walking in a mental fog that shut me down emotionally and I didn't even realize it. I drifted so far from where my relationship with the Lord should have been and yet, the Lord was good and He never let go. He always kept His hand on me. Somewhere in the midst of those years I realized that when the time came to write, it would be centered on my years with youth. I began blogging about my experiences; youth who impacted me; lots of tragedies. The truth is, there are many sad stories.

Sadly, my thinking became focused on the tragedies; all the things I saw that were unproductive and in fact, harmful in the youth service field. From self-righteousness grew condescension. I wanted to write about the skills involved and the mindset behind working with youth but as many times as I tried to write, the Lord shut it down.

By the time I had got myself into a tangled mess of self-righteousness and living life from that platform, I was shattered when it all came crashing down. One by one, each area of security in my life, was rendered insecure. Anxiety and panic attacks grew by the day. Not just in me but in that of my children as well. Day by day, as I worked to piece back together my life and be the mother I needed to be, two things began to take root in my heart.

The first being: I needed Jesus. Somehow in the midst

of my wandering I had ceased nurturing my own personal relationship with Jesus. I could not do anything without Him! Jesus became my life-line and I fell head over heels in love with Him. I have so many sweet memories of that time of healing.

The second thing was that it was time to take 25 years of youth work and put it to pen. That became a driving force that I committed to but, I was unable to write. I'd never had a problem with writing before so to face a wall I could not breach was disheartening. However, that wall was the catalyst to a deeper craving to serve the Lord in a new way. The drive to write only intensified as I hungered for more closeness to Him.

What I began to understanding was that He needed to direct my words and that would come as I let Him work in me. How had I strayed so far from Him? Many times, in those months as we worked to restore our home and family with healing, emotionally broken I cried out to the Lord to correct my heart. My prayer was two-fold. "Lord, I give you my 'yes' and I give you my heart. Please correct the attitude of my heart and the thoughts in my mind." He answered my prayer over and over again. Each time I saw another area I needed Him to correct my thinking and my heart, He did. Even when I did not know exactly what was wrong but only had the knowledge of *something* being there that should not be, He was faithful to reveal it to me and heal anew.

One of those times as I sat for the umpteenth time

trying to write and I felt like I had a muzzle on my writing voice, it came to me in a picture of a coin. I was writing from the wrong side of the coin. I began to realize that the Lord was telling me I was coming to the table from the wrong position. The closer I drew to Him the more the Lord began to heal me and shift my heart to compassion for my fellow youth workers and the easier it became to move my fingers.

Fast forward to a few days later as I was pondering the Lord's heart for His ministers, the Lord both affirmed the knowledge of His task for me and pulled the rug out from under it. The Holy Spirit impressed upon me, "Yes, Pearline you are correct but you are not coming at it from MY heart."

I realized then that I needed to come to a better understanding of the Lord's heart for his people who were serving and that my task was not to write about what I knew to be effective with youth. It was to come from another direction and I did not yet fully understand what that was yet. I needed to yield because He was waiting to write it *with* me as my partner.

I have always known that my life would be in the field I have been in. There was never a moment of doubt. The fire in my heart for youth burns even hotter know all these years later. Over and over He has positioned me for this task and I have embraced it but I was always doing it alone in my own strength. The knowledge that I did not have to write alone but that the Holy Spirit would write with me brought me a new level of calm, peace and security.

My position was an easy one from then on: to wait on Him, look for Him and He would lead the way. I yielded that day. I knew His promise that my years as a youth worker would be on pages someday. I also knew He would walk the process with me and bring me to where I needed to be to write.

Desperation for relief has a way of drawing you to the places you might not otherwise go. Early on, in the first week of 8-10 hour, days at a table studying and writing, I was in pain. Physical pain. I am an active woman who spends 16+ hours a day on her feet and works out regularly. To overnight halt that lifestyle and park her booty at a table with her eyes locked on a computer screen, a book, or paper was physically painful. I was not physically conditioned for it. My back was spasming, I was having muscle cramps all along my body. My headaches turned into migraines and my eyes were so blurry from fatigue and overuse I could no longer read anything.

Around 10 am on the 6th day even my hands were cramping. I could push through pain but I had to be able to see. I was frustrated and discouraged because the road was going to be long if I could not overcome the physical adjustment. I texted my mother and asked her to pray with me that the Holy Spirit would empower me physically to be able to perform. I needed my eye sight and I needed the cramping to stop. With tears of frustration I laid down on the couch on my belly. I resolved to take a nap and hopefully the change in position and closing my eyes would give me some reprieve so I could continue working. I laid there and said a prayer for supernatural rest and for empowering my body in a way that only He could in easing the pain and clearing my eyes. I couldn't see to set my alarm on my phone so I set what I thought was a 30-minute timer. As I laid the phone on the floor next to couch I felt my daughter very gently lay a blanket on me even to covering my head. My last thought was, "Aww…she put a blanket on me but why cover my head?" And…I was out cold the next second. I woke in an instant wide awake and stood up reaching out to grab the blanket as it fell.

There was no blanket.

I looked around thinking my daughter may have taken it off of me but that confused me because I had felt it on me when I woke seconds before. There was no blanket anywhere. I stood there recharged like a battery with new juice. Like I had slept 10 hours. No sleep haze. No grogginess. Not a single ache anywhere in my body. My eyesight was perfect. No burn, blur or heaviness. They were clearer than they had been in months! I picked up my cell off the floor wondering why the alarm had not gone off because obviously I had been asleep way too long.

It had been three minutes.

I must have stared at my phone for 10 seconds thoroughly confused. My daughter came walking through the room and seeing me standing there she said, "I thought you said you were going to take a nap."

"I did. Did you put a blanket on me?"

She looked at me like I had lost my mind and I kinda thought I had too. "Nooo…you gonna nap or what?"

"I DID!" That's when it dawned on me and I began laughing. "I did take a nap. Best nap I've ever had actually. A God nap. Back to work now." I headed back to the table feeling wonderful physically and like the Holy Spirit had given me kiss on the cheek with His gift. He had supercharged me.

The Lord did a lot of work on my sleep and in my sleep in the months of overcoming severe anxiety the year prior. He not only healed me of Insomnia but He purified my sleep. I used to hate waking in the morning because my thoughts were so tormented I dreaded it. The soft place of waking from a dream before the mind is fully conscious was a place of torment for me. One night in the fall of 16' I had prayed for the Lord to take over that window of my sleep cycle. I prayed that not only would the attack on my mind stop but I asked specifically that the Lord would talk to me in that window. I wanted my first greeting to be from Him and I asked Him for it.

Jesus said to become like little children and I took that to heart. I looked for Him in small places and in big places and I always found him. I found Him even in my sleep. From then on, the Lord brought me so much joy in my waking moments from REM sleep I grew to love it. It became the most precious time of day for me.

From the first day I committed to writing, as I woke the Lord spoke to me the scripture to begin in for that day. He led the way. As I would begin to come out of sleep I would wait for the Lord to reveal to me the scripture I would need. He would impress it upon my mind. It was so amazing! The Holy Spirit became my writing partner. At night if I had to stop someplace unfinished, I would write my prayer asking Him to guide me on that specific topic and the next morning I would remain soft eagerly awaiting His direction. First, the book of the Bible. Then, the chapter. It always came.

One night I went to sleep with a busy mind on what I was to cover the next day. I woke the next morning and waited for His direction. It came.

"Ephesians"

I waited for the chapter.

"Ephesians," came a second time.

I chuckled to myself, "Ok. Ephesians it is." I made my coffee and prepared to sit down to read all the while amused. He wanted me to read the whole book of Ephesians, so read it I would, and I did. Twice. It took me two hours to make my way through it because He was speaking to my heart so deeply. My prayer journal filled up by three more pages that morning. When I finally got around to writing I was blown away to find that everything I needed had been in

Ephesians. The Lord had power packed me in preparation for that day. So many nights I fell asleep at the table with a smile on my face because of what He had shown me in the process of writing this together. I could have never asked for a better study partner.

Every day He had a gift for me. One night, He beckoned me outside. It was an urgent call to go outside. It was well after sunset and I sat down in a lawn chair, put my earbuds in and played one of my favorite artists, Amanda Cook, on YouTube. I laid my head back and closed my eyes as a song I had never heard came on, "Our Breath Back."

I was completely leveled listening to it. That afternoon I had been journaling about overcoming anxiety, the restoration of clear breath and the knowledge that Jesus had been there with me. Here I was sitting in my backyard tears streaming down my face as I listened to Amanda sing so beautifully what had been in my heart that day. At times, word for word. Without thought I opened my eyes and turned to look to my right and in that second the most stunning shooting star soared across the night sky. Longer and brighter than any I had ever witnessed before. I felt Him then, "Just cause, I love you…"

The Holy Spirit drew me closer, day by day, in the writing process. Day after day He has been my constant companion. Day after day He has held my hand, whispered in my ear, wiped more tears from my face than anyone ever; He's walked more miles, sang me more songs, and woke me with a softly spoken word, danced with me, laughed with me and He has released me from the bondage of anxiety, lust, self-doubt, insecurity, unforgiveness and pride. He has shown me what agape is and what a Christ-like love is to look like in a man.

I am no longer afraid. He never gave me a spirit of fear but He gave me a Spirit of power, strength and of sound mind. He changed my life and there is no turning back now. There's work to be done. In me cause I still have a seriously long way to go and as His servant there is much to do for others. My passion for our youth is not the same now as it was all those years ago when I began. Its deeper; wider. Some days it will stop me in my tracks as I realize the future ahead of them if change does not come. I see the impact of technology to the generation we have today and it concerns me greatly. Sexual promiscuity, identity confusion, narcotics, alcoholism, pornography, aggression and negativity are rampant.

However, I see the presence of the Creator everywhere I walk. Time and time again the Lord has shown himself faithful in the lives of the most hardest hearts, starting in mine. He never gives up. He is a God of miracles! He is there…always. Sometimes it's nothing more than, "Hi Miss!" and the wave of greeting that comes with it. Sometimes it's when I have the profound honor of sharing a scripture with someone who has not heard one before. Thankfully, God is still in our schools and with our youth today and we are so blessed we see Him working there.

"I have said these things to you, that in me you may have peace. In the world you will have tribulation. But take heart; I have overcome the world." John 16:33

Printed in the United States
By Bookmasters